❖❖❖ SUPERHINTS ❖❖❖
FOR COOKS

From the Famous, the Professional and
Those Who Entertain

Compiled by
The Lady Wardington

MICHAEL JOSEPH
LONDON

Michael Joseph Ltd

Published by the Penguin Group
27 Wrights Lane, London W8 5TZ
Viking Penguin Inc., 375 Hudson Street, New York, New York 10014, USA
Penguin Books Australia Ltd, Ringwood, Victoria, Australia
Penguin Books Canada Ltd, 10 Alcorn Avenue, Toronto, Ontario,
Canada M4V 3B2
Penguin Books (NZ) Ltd, 182–190 Wairau Road, Auckland 10,
New Zealand

Penguin Books Ltd, Registered Offices: Harmondsworth,
Middlesex, England

First published in Great Britain October 1994
Second impression before publication October 1994

Printed in Great Britain by
Butler & Tanner Ltd
Frome and London

ISBN 0 7181 3820 1

Note:
The hints in this book are intended to suggest possible solutions only.
While every effort has been made to check their accuracy, the compiler,
contributors and publisher can neither guarantee absolute success nor
accept any legal responsibility or liability for their effectiveness.

Hints vary in the amount of detailed quantities and method given
and some assume knowledge of cooking techniques. If in doubt, an
experienced cook should use his/her own judgement; a less experienced
cook will probably find enough assistance in any general cookery book.
When measuring ingredients, follow either metric or imperial systems, not
a mixture.

❖❖❖ Contents ❖❖❖

FOREWORD

The Katharine House Hospice, which receives all the royalties from this book and bears none of the expense, opened in 1991, and is one of the youngest independent hospices. It was conceived in 1984 when Neil Gadsby's only daughter died tragically young and he realized the need for terminal care for cancer patients in the Banbury area.

Now the attractive building, standing in lovely grounds, looks after over 200 people a year, either as day patients or in one of the pretty rooms which open on to the garden. All this costs money: £1 a minute, which is where this book makes a real contribution.

This is my third 'Superhints' book and none of them would have been possible without the active encouragement of Jane Evans, who pushed on helping me to find a publisher when I was losing heart, and Laurie Purden, who taught me how to get the book together properly. I am so grateful to them. They both knew Marion Shaw whose death inspired me to help the Hospice – and oh, how she would have enjoyed the hunt for hints.

It has been a fascinating exercise. The kindness and creativity of friends, acquaintances and total strangers who have taken so much time and trouble to think of hints has been wonderful.

The profusion of hints and ingenuity of ideas so generously donated, often from people who have had personal experience of hospice care, has made the task of compiling this book a joy. I know it isn't easy to think of a 'hint' and I'm deeply appreciative of the thought that has gone into so many of the contributions. I just wish that space had allowed me to include every single one.

Opening the post every morning has been a constant source of excitement – and amazement. The single most astonishing factor has been the total absence of any thought of economy – perhaps symptomatic of a society which buys more books than they borrow from the library. I had planned a nice section on 'Left-overs' but only two hints out of nearly 600 qualified in that area. So the sections arranged themselves – the range of subjects covered giving lots of variety.

The eccentric and amusing hints are impossible to resist, such as the advice in rhyme for cooking a swan, which can surely be of interest only to the Queen, and Derek Nimmo's swashbuckling system of removing champagne corks, not to mention Victoria Wood's way of dealing with a disastrous dinner party.

Some of the resourceful and ingenious hints have changed my life, such as Mrs Boughey's discovery that you can make a soufflé in the morning and cook it at night, Ken Goody's foolproof method of cooking a salmon and Michael Barry's way with pasta, which he's not ashamed to admit he got off the back of a packet – and as a cook-hostess myself I thought Max Hastings' philosophical hint definitely hit the spot.

Thank you for buying this book. I hope you'll enjoy these tips and wrinkles and benefit from the ideas – and only occasionally feel the urge to follow the Duchess of Devonshire's advice to get someone else to cook for you.

Audrey Wardington

STARTERS AND SOUPS

*My idea of heaven is eating pâté de foie gras
to the sound of trumpets.*

REVD SIDNEY SMITH

GOOD CIRCULATION

If you're entertaining a large or mixed group such
as at Christmas or a dinner before a dance, serve
good cocktail eats (dilled salmon, filo parcels)
instead of a first course. This has the double
advantage of allowing guests to circulate round
more people than they would when seated and
also saves laying and washing-up a whole course.

Lady Edmonstone

CANAPÉS

That lovely long French loaf that has lost its
charm the next day can be transformed to be the
base for glamorous canapés. Cut it into ½-inch
(1.25 cm)-thick slices, brush each side with olive
oil, sprinkle with salt, and lightly grill them – on a
rack so that they don't soften. They can be stored
in an air-tight tin and topped with anchovies
scattered with capers, grilled Mediterranean
vegetables or whatever when you have a party.

Lorna Wing
Caterer

ITTY-BITTY

This simple mixture makes lots of delicious cheesy nibbles, biscuity and crisp. All you do is cream 4 oz (100 g) butter with 4 oz (100 g) grated mature Cheddar cheese. Add 2 cups of plain flour, 4 oz (100 g) of Rice Krispies, a teaspoon of salt and a teaspoon of cayenne pepper. Form into small balls and place on baking trays, flatten and cook at Gas mark 4, 350°F (180°C) for about 10 minutes.

Suzie Colling

PEAR-SHAPED

Fruit and cheese is as good a combination at the start of a meal as it is at the end. Take a ripe pear per person, peel, halve and hollow them out. Brush with lemon juice to stop them discolouring if they are to be kept waiting. Fill with Stilton mashed with a little thick cream, put the halves together and paint with some more lemon juice. Finally, roll in crushed nuts before serving.

Mrs Allen Muschamp

PEAR-SHAPED AGAIN

Pears and prawns go together well. Peel and halve the fruit, allowing half a pear per person, and scoop out the middle. Wipe over with lemon juice to stop them going brown if they are to wait long. Mix some small prawns with a little mayonnaise and pile in the middle. *Voilà* – a perfect first course.

Richard Vanderpump

PAIRED PEARS

Arrange alternate slices of peeled, ripe avocado pears and dessert pears on individual plates, add a slice or two of Parma ham and serve with a chive and chervil vinaigrette and warm Italian or French bread.

Geraldene Holt
Food writer

GREEN LIGHT

A vinaigrette dressing whizzed up in the blender with a bunch of watercress, so that it becomes bright green, drizzled over avocados, sliced and laid fan-wise on a plate, adds flavour as well as colour to this first course.

Agnes Taylor
Volunteer fundraiser, Katharine House Hospice

TOPPING

Oeufs en Cocottes are an excellent starter for a lunch party and my mother's cook made the best sauce for them – it has always been one of our favourites and it's so easy. Combine tomato ketchup and single cream 50/50, heat and pour over the baked eggs.

Marchioness of Tavistock

JAM WITH IT

An ordinary Ardennes pâté will be transformed if it is served topped with damson preserve.

Iris Murdoch
Author

BACON AND CRAB STICKS

For a delicious and easy starter – or possibly savoury – wrap a slice of smoked streaky bacon round a crab stick and bake for about ten minutes in a medium oven. Serve at least two per person, either plain, on toast, or with one of your favourite sauces.

Lady Owen

FORGET THE DIET

This is a first course I prepare for a shooting lunch. Forget it if your friends are on a diet. For four people you will need: 1 lb (½ kg) waxy potatoes, 1 lb (½ kg) mushrooms (preferably *porcini*), 2½ oz (60 g) butter, a clove of garlic, 2½ oz (60 g) grated Parmesan, single cream to cover, 4 eggs and seasoning to taste.

Boil the potatoes and slice them. Slice the mushrooms – in an ideal world these should be the special Italian *porcini* but they are seasonal so ordinary field ones may have to do – and fry them in butter with the clove of garlic for 20 minutes. Remove garlic. Butter a fireproof dish, put in a layer of potatoes sprinkled with Parmesan cheese and cover it with a layer of mushrooms. You may then have another layer of potatoes etc., if you wish; then another layer of potatoes etc. All this can be done well in advance. Make indentations in the surface, sprinkle with more Parmesan cheese and break the eggs into the dents. Cover everything with cream. Pop into a hot oven (Gas mark 6, 400°F (200°C)) for about 10 minutes or longer if you like your eggs well cooked. It is very much a matter of individual taste so perhaps you should practise on the family first.

Lady Dashwood

WAFER-THIN

The secret to cutting wafer-thin brown bread and butter, the perfect accompaniment to smoked salmon, is to half-freeze the loaf. This way it can be buttered and cut very thin without converting half the loaf into a useless pile of doorsteps and crumbs.

Mrs Douglas Hurd

ATTENTION TO DETAIL

Caviare is such a treat that it is essential to have everything that goes with it just right. For perfect toast use frozen, already sliced white bread and turn the toaster to a higher setting, thus achieving a crisp outside while the middle remains soft.

The Lord Wardington

CAVIARE SPECIAL

Always rinse red caviare in half a cup of water. It absorbs the excess salt and makes the caviare twice as delicious.

Duncan Fallowell

TRULY SPOILING

For a seriously luxurious starter try a caviare terrine. Line a terrine with foil and cover the bottom with a layer of caviare (in fact, lump fish roe will do). On to this pack a layer of chopped hard-boiled egg mixed with a little melted butter, then a layer of chopped chives and finally sour cream or yoghurt stiffened with cream cheese. Press it all down well and put it in the fridge for a few hours. Turn it out carefully and either slice it before it goes to the table or let your guests help themselves.

Mrs Neil Petrie

... A triple thickness of narrow foil in the base of a terrine dish – long enough to lift out – makes removing the terrine an easy job.

Mrs Cherry Palmer

... When I'm making a terrine I always line it with cling film. This stops anything sticking to the side.

Kevin Mangeolles
Head Chef, Michaels Nook, Grasmere

11

SPEEDY

The quickest first course to prepare – though you have to start several hours before the meal – is *consommé en gelée* topped with sour cream and lump fish roe. Pour the consommé (I use Crosse and Blackwell's – it seems to gel best) into suitable glasses and put them in the fridge so that the soup will set. Then all you have to do is spoon on sour cream to cover the consommé and top it with a teaspoonful of lump fish roe.

Sara Carter
Manageress, Katharine House Hospice Shop, Banbury

NOT FOR TEETOTALLERS

If you pride yourself on the excellence of your Bloody Mary, why not turn it into a really snappy starter for a lunch or dinner? Make it into a jelly, by heating about 6 tablespoons of the drink and adding powdered gelatine. When it has completely dissolved mix it into the rest of the Bloody Mary (1½ packets of gelatine to 1 pint (600ml) of Bloody Mary) and either pour it into ramekins or a ring mould. When set, turn out, garnish with watercress and warn any teetotal guests of the alcoholic content.

The Lady Wardington

HOT FAVOURITE

The vital ingredient for this mousse sounds peculiar. It is horseradish. I was tremendously impressed when we first had it and now it has become a regular starter. As I understand it, you make a lightly flavoured savoury mousse and just before it sets stir in freshly grated horseradish, tasting as you add to get the flavour to your liking – we like ours

strong . We serve it with a carrot and tomato sauce
to give a bit of colour.

Rt. Hon. Michael Heseltine MP

THIN SLICES

Carpaccio – very, very thin slices of raw beef – is
probably best cut for you by the butcher on his
bacon slicer. But if this is impractical, the answer
is to half-freeze the meat before slicing it yourself.

Arabella Boxer
Food writer

INVIGORATING BROTH

For a really invigorating broth, quick to make,
grate an onion and a carrot and place in a
saucepan with a bay leaf, a twig of thyme, a clove
of garlic and 4 oz (100 g) of raw chopped beef.
Cover with 1½ pints (900 ml) cold water, bring to
the boil, reduce the heat and simmer for an hour,
covered. Pass through a sieve and serve, sprinkled
with minced parsley and finely shredded raw
carrot. You may like to add some sautéed shallots
just before serving for extra flavour.

Mireille Johnston
Food writer

SAD SALAD SOUP

Do you know what to do with a dressed green
salad which hasn't been used up? Simply add peas,
a couple of chopped onions and 1½ pints (600 ml)
chicken stock, boil and liquidize into soup. It is
delicious and known as Delectable Pea and Sad
Salad Soup.

Miranda Hall
Cordon bleu demonstrator

13

TOO MUCH

Faced with a glut of lettuce, make soup. Soften a cup of chopped potatoes and the same amount of onions in 2 oz (50 g) of butter, cooking slowly in their own steam in a covered saucepan. Add 2 pt (1.2 litres) stock and boil until really soft, then throw in three or more cups of chopped lettuce and boil for a minute or two. Purée and add a tablespoon of chopped mint, 2–3 tablespoons of cream or milk and season carefully.

Myrtle Allen
Chef and Proprietor, Ballymaloe House, County Cork

WASTE NOT

Don't throw away those green leek tops. Trim off any brown or very tough leaves, slice them vertically, soak them in cold water and rinse thoroughly. Peel and chop a couple of potatoes and onions and sweat in 2 oz (50 g) butter, then add the leek tops to sweat for a little longer. Pour on about 2 pt (1.2 litres) of homemade chicken stock, bring to the boil, then reduce the heat and simmer, covered, for 20–30 minutes. Liquidize – Vichyssoise! Delicious and economical.

Derek Waring
Actor

SUPER SOUP

This soup is really our standard winter lunch. We never tire of it and get endless variety by varying the ingredients. Chop tomatoes, broccoli, avocado, carrots and any other vegetable you fancy, in whatever quantities you wish, into a tin or packet of vegetable soup. Add some extra stock or water, boil it up and cook until the vegetables

14

are tender. Add a couple of tablespoons of mango chutney and stir well. It's nice with a spoonful of natural yoghurt added on serving.

Chris Bonington
Mountaineer

A DEFINITE IMPROVEMENT

When a soup is bland or worse, especially in British Rail restaurant cars, add a little sugar. And hardly any soups fail to taste better for a splosh of Cognac and a good squeeze of lemon.

The Marquess of Anglesey

THE FINAL TOUCH

As a final addition to your cooked recipe when you have made pumpkin soup, try adding a tub of Mascarpone cheese. You will have a delicious-tasting soup every time.

Mrs Bill Tidy
Food writer

CLEAR RED

Borsch, lovely clear red beetroot soup, can sometimes have a cloying sweetness to it. Counter this with some of the juice from pickled beetroots – or, if you don't have any in your cupboard, try a teaspoonful or two of vinegar.

Mrs Kenneth Harper

BEER IS BEST

When you make French onion soup add some heavy draught beer. It really gives it another flavour dimension.

Kate Hewitt
Volunteer receptionist, Katharine House Hospice

GREEN, GREEN

When you make watercress soup, bring the chopped cress to the boil in a little salted water. Strain it (the water can go in the soup). Blend the cress to a purée with a little cold water and add it to the finished soup at the last minute. This provides not only a fresher flavour but a lovely vivid colour.

Roger Pergl-Wilson
Chef and Proprietor, Rogers, Windermere

BETTER FOR YOU

Instead of thickening soups and stews with a roux of flour and butter, use puréed root vegetables such as potatoes and parsnips – thus reducing the calorie value and adding extra flavour.

Dr Eileen Barratt
Nutritionist, Inglewood Health Hydro, Kintbury

OFF WITH THE FAT

If there is a thick layer of fat on the surface of a hot soup, drop 4 or 5 ice-cubes into it. Have ready a slotted draining spoon to fish them out immediately – the solidified fat will have adhered to the ice-cubes. Be quick, otherwise the cubes will begin to melt and dilute the soup. Repeat if necessary.

Patrick Anthony
TV chef

KEEP YOUR COOL

Just as one would never serve a hot soup in a cold bowl, we at the restaurant always chill our soup bowls in the fridge before serving. Especially in the summer, this really does add a special touch to the presentation of the meal.

Sally Clarke
Cook and Proprietor, Clarke's, London

WHAT, NO DRIP

Transferring soup from saucepan to bowl can be a messy business with drips between the two. To avoid this, fill the ladle and lightly touch the bottom of its bowl upon the surface of the soup in the saucepan before pouring. No drips!

Lady Martha Ponsonby

CROÛTONS GALORE

Here's a quick and easy way to make a lot of croûtons for soups and salads. Cut the crust off a large sliced white loaf and cut into croûton-sized dice. Melt ½ lb (225 g) butter and pour it into a large mixing bowl. Add the bread, season and mix well. Spread on to two large baking trays and cook in the top of a pre-heated oven at Gas mark 6, 400°F (200°C) for about 30 minutes. The outside ones will cook more quickly so move these to the middle and the others to the outside half-way through: you may need a little longer to get them really crisp and brown. Cool on kitchen paper and store in air-tight jars.

Ruby Nag
Anglo-Bulgarian home help

... If you like Parmesan croûtons, sprinkle the oiled cubes with grated Parmesan cheese and toss in oil again before cooking.

Lindsay Bareham
Food writer

... And for economy, save the crusts cut from sandwiches, trim into neat little pieces and use for croûtons.

Philippa Davenport
Food and cookery writer, Financial Times
and Country Living

FISH DISHES

*'Turbot, Sir?' said the waiter, placing before me
two fish bones, two eyeballs and a bit of black
mackintosh.*

THOMAS EARLE WELBY

FRESHER LONGER

Fish really must be fresh to be perfect, but it has
always been a problem to keep it that way. But
now the vac-pac has entered our lives. Most good
fishmongers have a machine which will seal your
purchase into a vacuum pack so that it will keep
absolutely fresh for at least two days without
making the fridge smelly – and you can slip it
straight into the freezer without having to bother
with freezer bags.

Lynda Brown
Food writer

TESTING, TESTING

To tell whether fish or meat has been frozen, squeeze a piece of the flesh between forefinger and thumb. If an excess of liquid appears, you can be fairly certain that it has been frozen.

Mike Womersley
Head Chef, Luckham Park, Colerne

A COLD FISH

Here is my way – I find it foolproof – of cooking fresh salmon to serve cold. Place it in a pan of cold water with salt and a little olive oil and bring it slowly to the boil. Let it bubble up twice, remove from the heat and leave the fish in the water to cool overnight. The fresh, moist result will surprise you.

Ken Goody
Chef and Proprietor, The Cemlyn, Harlech

DISHWASHER COOKED

Wrap a nice big salmon carefully in two layers of foil, place it on a platter and put it in the dishwasher. Turn the machine on to the hottest programme and let it run the full cycle. When you take it out it will be perfectly cooked – and there will be no washing up!

Sue Crewe
Journalist

DON'T CUT THE MUSTARD

To make a dish of delicious mackerel, top and tail the fish, halve them and remove the backbones. Sprinkle with sea salt and black pepper and smear really thickly with good Dijon mustard. Cook with a little oil in a thick shallow pan. The mustard is the key to this dish.

The Marchioness of Salisbury

POACHED

In the past I have poached quenelles in water but I felt that they lost some of their flavour. Now I cook them in fish stock and find this much better.

Carmen Lleô
Professional cook

NO ODOUR

This is the way I cook fish for a recipe such as fishcakes – or even for the cat! Prepare the fish and put it in a pan with a tight-fitting lid. Pour on boiling water, fit on the lid and leave to cool. The fish is then ready for use with no smell all over the house.

Ms E. Woodford

... I find that if I rub a few drops of sesame oil into the cavity of the fish there is no odour while it is cooking – particularly with carp.

Annie Morley-Slim
Cookery teacher, Westminster Adult Education Service

... The smell of fish cooking can pervade the whole house. If, when you're steaming it, you place a piece of stale bread over it the bread will absorb all the odours and your house will be fish-free.

HKH Princess Lilian of Sweden

... A teaspoon of sliced ginger root added to fish and seafood dishes helps to neutralize fishy odours.

Siew Choo Calthorpe
Cookery teacher, Westminster Adult Education Service

THE ULTIMATE FISHCAKE

Instead of mixing cooked flaked fish with mashed

potato to make fishcakes in the classic manner, substitute béchamel sauce for the potato. You must make the sauce thicker than you would normally, add the fish to it when it is hot and pour the mixture on to a greased tray. Allow it to cool and refrigerate for several hours until set. Shape the cakes, flour them and coat with breadcrumbs, then fry them until golden brown. These fishcakes will be much lighter and more tasty than if they were made with potatoes.

Michael Hasler
Head Chef, Mark's Club, London

NOT SO DUSTY

When dusting fish, meat, poultry or vegetables with flour, put a little flour in a plastic bag, put the piece of food inside and tie up the opening. Gently shake the bag until the food is covered. This saves a lot of mess and is especially useful if you have a small working area.

Willi Elsener
Executive Chef, The Dorchester, London

BE FREE WITH THE PARSLEY

People are often mean with parsley, despite its availability. Use at least a cupful with kedgeree – added near the end. It looks lovely and gives a wonderful fresh taste.

Mrs John Biffen

SALT

Season fish immediately *after* cooking. Salt will dry the fish too much if added beforehand, removing moisture and making it difficult to handle.

Nick Nairn
Chef and Proprietor, Braeval Old Mill, Stirling

COMPLEMENTARY FLAVOURS

Try using vegetable stock in sauces for fish dishes, rather than fish stock. The flavours can be more complementary.

David Wilson
Chef and Proprietor, The Peat Inn, Cupar

TROUT WITH ALMONDS

Fry a trout in a little oil and butter with some blanched almonds; allow five minutes each side. Take out the trout and pour some cream and a generous splash of Pernod into the pan. Swirl around to mix with the juices and pour over the trout.

Lucy Gutteridge
Actress

ADD OIL

A hint from my husband's French mother: when heating butter for frying or making a sauce or whatever, always add a little oil. It will prevent the butter from burning and if you use a light one (not olive oil) there will be no difference to the taste.

Lady Barbirolli

IF YOU DON'T LIKE THE HEAT …

To bring the heat down quickly in a deep-fat fryer, put in a whole potato.

Ruth Watson
Chef and Proprietor, The Fox and Goose Inn, Fressingfield

BETTER BATTER

This must be the quickest batter to make for fish

22

and chips, and it is always crispy. Mix together 10 fl oz (300 ml) of lager with 8 oz (250 g) of self-raising flour, season with salt and pepper and it is ready to use.

Gary Rhodes
Head Chef, The Greenhouse, London

ALMOST KOSHER

If a recipe calls for fish fillets – or whole fish – to be shallow-fried, having been rolled in seasoned flour, try substituting seasoned Matzo Meal for the flour. You will find the finished fish both crisper and more attractive-looking. Matzo Meal is used a great deal in Jewish cookery and is available from good delicatessens.

Richard Stein
Chef and Proprietor, The Seafood Restaurant, Padstow

GREAT COMBINATION

I love to experiment and I have come up with what I think is a brand new combination. On a finger of fresh brown buttered bread lay a sliver of apple with a squeeze of lemon juice. Cover that with smoked salmon liberally sprinkled with freshly ground black pepper. A fascinating blend of flavours. Serve with an aperitif.

Richard Good
Merchant banker

SWALLOWED A BONE?

If anyone gets a fish bone stuck in their throat, make them swallow a mouthful of malt vinegar – the bone will dissolve immediately.

The Marchioness of Zetland

SHUCKS!

Opening oysters – 'shucking' in professional parlance – can be a difficult business. We had to open 350 for a party the other night, to be poached with a sauce. We thought we would experiment and took the plunge, literally. We dipped the fresh, unopened oysters into a huge pan of boiling water for ten seconds then instantly cooled them in cold water. The oysters were perfectly cooked, retaining their shape, and the shells were open. Served with a sauce of whipped cream, *crème fraîche* and mayonnaise mixed with chives, they were sensational.

Patrick McDonald
Chef and Proprietor, Epicurian, Cheltenham

WATCH THE POT

It is vitally important, when cooking shellfish, not to overcook, or to allow the stock to boil, in which case the flesh will become rubbery and tough.

Raymond Blanc
Chef and Proprietor, Le Manoir aux Quat'Saisons,
Great Milton

JOINTS, STEWS, POULTRY AND GAME

....delicious, nourishing and wholesome food, whether stewed, roasted or baked, and I make no doubt that it will equally serve in a fricase or a ragout.

JONATHAN SWIFT, *A Modest Proposal*

OVERNIGHT STAY

Most beef or lamb joints are improved by spending the night (or at least a few hours) in a polythene bag with chopped onion, garlic, herbs and red wine. The mixture can then be added to the gravy.

Mrs J. E. H. Collins

RELAXATION

Always leave roasted joints of meat to 'rest' after cooking. This will help the meat to achieve an even colour throughout and help it to 'relax'.

Keith Marshall
Chef and Proprietor, The Dew Pond, Old Burghclere

JUICY

Before roasting a joint, season it and fry it on top of the stove, sealing all sides before placing it in the oven. This keeps in the juices of the meat when it is cooking and gives it a much better flavour in the end.

Robert Lyons
Resident Director, The Bay Horse Inn, Ulverston

PINCHED FROM PROVENCE

To enhance the flavour of roast meat, adopt the Provençal habit of adding a head or two of garlic, separated into unpeeled cloves, to the roasting pan during the last half hour of cooking. Serve the mellow-flavoured garlic alongside the carved meat.

Geraldene Holt
Food writer

CUT AND COME AGAIN

To feed four people, take a 4–5 lb (2–2.5 kg) leg of lamb and with a sharp knife make 7 or 8 slits in the meat. Squeeze the juice from 4 lemons and add it to 2 tablespoons of wine vinegar, 2 tablespoons of olive oil, Dijon mustard to taste, salt and pepper. Smooth this sauce, which shouldn't be too thin, all over the lamb, especially in the slits. Place a small clove of garlic in each slit and cover the whole with rosemary. Place in a domed Webber barbecue over a very low heat – or into a low oven, Gas mark 2, 300°F (150°C) – for approximately 3–3½ hours, basting regularly with the remaining sauce.

For two people, cook the same amount, because they will always come back for more!

David Suchet
Actor

IN THE BAG

Where possible, when marinating, use a plastic bag. Clip it closed securely and keep it near to hand, turning it from time to time during the day. Use the liquid for a sauce.

The Countess of Minto

INJECTION

When there isn't time to leave meat to marinate properly ask a favourite nurse for a syringe and inject the marinade into the meat.

Alan Root

NEW BROOMS

Make a little broom of sprigs of rosemary, thyme and any other herbs one has handy and use it to baste a roast, dipping it into the fat and brushing it over the meat. It gives a special flavour to the joint.

The Lady Glenconner

PAINTING

Always keep a decorator's paintbrush – the sort with which you might paint a windowframe rather than a wall – to hand in the kitchen for basting. Any roast, grilled fish or meat can be quickly wiped over with fat – far easier than pouring it over with a spoon.

Lord Montagu of Beaulieu

SNAP CRACKLE

Pork crackling *must* be crisp to be edible – nothing is more depressing than a rubbery outside to a loin of pork. Here is the foolproof way to make it perfect every time. Have the skin deeply scored and place the joint, skin side down, into a roasting tin an inch deep in boiling water. Put into a very hot (Gas mark 8, 450°F (230°C)) oven and cook for 15 minutes. Remove from the oven, pour off the liquid and rub salt well in to the skin. Roast, skin side up at Gas mark 4, 350°F (180°C) for 30 minutes to the pound. If the loin has been boned and rolled, place the tin with about an inch of water in it on top of the stove on a high heat and sear the skin, turning the joint to ensure total sealing.

Obby Waller
Interior designer

BACHELOR TRICKS

Since I am now a bachelor, it might seem surprising that I seek out big rolled-rib joints at the supermarket. I look for those which don't have too much fat and cut them into steaks – easily done with a sharp knife. I wrap these individually and store them in the freezer. They are often better meat than you get when you buy individual steaks and work out much cheaper.

Duncan McEuan

YORKSHIRE SPECIAL

To make a decent Yorkshire pudding – a rare accomplishment south of Sheffield – you need two heaped tablespoons of plain flour and two eggs which you beat together until they are smooth. Mix in a pinch of salt and 6 fl oz (180 ml) of milk. This can be done two hours beforehand, but just before you use it add a tablespoon of ice-cold water. Put a baking tin with 2 tablespoons of vegetable oil into a very hot oven Gas mark 8, 450°F (230°C) for ten minutes, add the mixture and cook for 15 minutes. If you come from Yorkshire you will, of course, eat this as a starter rather than as an addition to the main course.

Rt. Hon. Dame Angela Rumbold MP

ON THE GRAVY TRAIN

Lift the taste of Yorkshire pudding by adding a special gravy. Chop two or three onions finely and allow them to cook slowly in a little butter until they have caramelized, then mix in a little gravy to moisten. When the puddings are cooked, pour a little onion gravy into the centre of each one and serve.

Gary Rhodes
Head Chef, The Greenhouse, London

… To add dark, rich colour and a robust flavour to a flat-tasting gravy, dissolve a little instant coffee powder in it.

Head Brownell

… Unsweetened cocoa powder gives gravy a special flavour – it's particularly good with game – and a rich colour, too.

Mrs Gerhard Bülle

… When making gravy from the meat juices in the pan, splash in the left-overs from the teapot for a fine colour and an elusive herby flavour (Lapsang is lovely).

Elisabeth Luard
Food columnist, The Scotsman

… Use cornflour instead of flour in gravy. Mix a teaspoonful in a cup with a little cold water and add it right at the end after everything has been reduced – and stir well or it will go lumpy. Cook for a minute and serve.

Sophie Conran

… In the marmalade season, buy some extra Seville oranges and store them in the freezer. Their juice makes a wonderful addition to the gravy for any game, and to sauces for fish and chicken. They thaw quickly and can then be squeezed in the usual way.

Simone Sekers
Food writer

… At Christmas, or when you have a lot of people to cater for, make your gravy early and keep it piping hot in a large thermos flask.

Miranda Hall
Cordon bleu demonstrator

RICH COLOUR

Cook your steak and kidney in Guinness. It gives a lovely dark colour and a very rich flavour.

The Marchioness of Zetland

GOOD GOULASH

It is my belief that whatever recipe one uses for a goulash, one should *always* have the same weight of onions as of meat – and the onions should be cooked gently before being added to the rest of the ingredients.

Octavian von Hofmannsthal
Art publisher

DISENTANGLE THE FAT

The problem of removing fat from oxtail – or any equally greasy casserole– was solved for us by Jane Grigson. Cook it as per your preferred recipe the day before you wish to eat it. Before cooling, however, strain the juice off the meat and other gubbins and chill them separately. The fat then doesn't get tangled up with the meat and veg and can be lifted cleanly off as a solid tablet the next day, before reuniting the ingredients and reheating.

Ian Carmichael
Actor

DON'T BE MEAN

When cooking Coq au Vin don't stint on the *vin*. Use a good half bottle of the roughest red you can find.

Charles Campbell
Restaurateur

BACK TO BACK

To roast a chicken thoroughly, place the largest end (i.e. the breast) towards the rear of the oven. The temperature at this point is at its hottest and the chicken will roast evenly.

Ian Mansfield
Head Chef, Eastwell Manor, Ashford

FULLER FLAVOUR

For a roast chicken with extra flavour, ease the skin away from the legs and breast and insert thyme, slivers of garlic and fresh green ginger. Use any or all of them to baste the bird while cooking.

Mrs John Biffen

STUFF IT

Get your friendly butcher to bone out a bird (chicken, quail, pheasant, guinea fowl, duck, etc.) for you, stuff it yourself and freeze it. Several fowl are as easy as one, while you're at it, and will provide ready-made meals when last-minute entertaining is required. Cook in foil with tarragon, a little white wine, seasoning and a knob of butter; serve with a green salad and new potatoes.

Jane Crosswell-Jones
Cookery instructor, Cookery at the Grange, Whatley

JUICY

In order to save the juices from a chicken or joint, cook it in a roasting bag – which actually improves the flavour – piercing the bag at the top. When the joint is cooked, lift it out, having cut the bag along the top only, and let the juices drain away into the roasting tin. Put them through a sieve into a bowl and chill. Once the layer of fat has solidified, remove it and you will be left with the maximum amount of pure stock.

John Junkin
Actor

GET STUFFED

Take trouble with stuffing. It is either made to tart up an unremarkable or tasteless ingredient like a marrow, or to make something expensive and exotic, like a quail, go further. At its best, stuffing is like getting the present at the end of 'Pass the Parcel'. It should be wonderful – a complementary but contrasting taste and texture. At its worst it is as if someone has emptied the sink tidy into your dinner.

A. A. Gill
Food writer and journalist

SUCCULENT

That dry, sandpapery texture that turkey can so easily acquire can be avoided. About forty-five minutes before cooking is finished, take your aluminium foil off the bird (to brown it) and at the same time, add about six tablespoons of water to the roasting tin. From then on, make sure that the liquid never quite dries up. The flesh will retain its moisture even when it's cooked through and through.

The Hon. Mrs Charles Kitchener

LEGS OFF

Always detach the legs and thighs from the Christmas turkey and cook them for an hour at Gas mark 5, 375°F (190°C) before putting the rest of the turkey in the oven. Butter it well and baste it thoroughly, cooking it breast up for 20 minutes, breast down for 40 minutes. This cooks the legs thoroughly and leaves the breast very moist – and it's easier to carve.

Lady Cazalet

USE A SHOVEL

We always have an enormous turkey on Christmas Day – too big, but my husband says it's easier to carve. Getting it from the roasting tin to the serving dish used to be a nightmare but now it's a doddle. We wash a big garden shovel and scoop it up with that.

The Lady Wardington

EAT IT UP

A roast goose can make a welcome change from turkey at Christmas, but be sure that it all gets eaten up while it is hot – a 10 lb (5 kg) bird will feed eight people – because, in my opinion, cold roast goose is *disgusting*.

Charles Wheeler

COOKED THE GOOSE

So often one hears people saying that they don't like eating roast goose because it is too fatty. If when cooking the bird you keep pricking the flesh so that the fat runs out, you will have a succulent, non-fatty roast to serve.

Mrs John Boughey

HORSEY, HORSEY

A roast goose will give an astonishing amount of fat. More than enough for culinary needs. But don't throw it away. Take it round to the nearest stable where they will use it for the treatment of various strains, sprains and bruises. It is particularly useful for its penetrative power. Smeared on injured joints it is an equine cure-all.

Timothy Rootes
Racehorse breeder

THE DAY AFTER

Left-over goose can be delicious in a sauce. Remove the meat from the carcass and dice it. Break up the bones and use them to make a well-flavoured stock. Fry a finely chopped large onion and stir in a teaspoon of tomato purée and about a dessertspoon of flour. Cook over a gentle heat for 1 minute, then gradually add 1 pt (600 ml) of the

34

stock. Bring to the boil, then simmer for about 15 minutes and stir in a tablespoon of mushroom ketchup.

Put the diced meat in a shallow dish and stir in the sauce with 2 tablespoons of port and a tablespoon of redcurrant jelly. Cover and heat gently and just before serving stir in a little cream and 4 oz (100 g) chopped *porcini* mushrooms.

Roy Thomas
Cook to Mr Timothy Rootes

JUST DUCKY

I know that if you want a crispy duck *really* crispy, you should roast it over a pan of water to draw off the fat – and there still won't be enough to go round!

Maureen Lipman
Actress and author

EXTENSION

Make a roast duck go further by roasting a boned piece of belly pork, skin scored, alongside the duck. Serve with the duck and no one will know the difference.

Mary Berry
Cookery writer, broadcaster and TV demonstrator

THE RIGHT HEIGHT

Pheasants are pleasantly 'hung' when the little wing feathers pluck easily, and highly so when the tail feathers pull out easily.

Rabbits are easier and less repellent to skin while they are still warm.

Mary Goldring
Freelance economist

PLUCKY

It is easier to pluck a pheasant if you plunge the bird into boiling water for a few moments after it has been hung – the feathers come away more easily and they don't make such a mess flying around.

June Zetter
Housekeeper

OVER THE TOP

If a game bird has gone a bit too high – even a little green round the edges – don't despair. It can be restored to edibility by a twenty-minute bath in vinegar. In fact, it will become more succulent after this treatment.

Lord Montagu of Beaulieu

BURGHLEY HOUSE PHEASANT

For a really delicious and different pheasant dish, take a hen bird and carefully lift the skin away from the breast. In a frying pan sauté 2 oz (50 g) chopped onions, 2 oz (50 g) mushrooms, some pine nuts, 2 oz (50 g) bacon, a dessertspoon of chopped preserved stem ginger and a clove of garlic until the onions are translucent and the bacon cooked. In another pan cook 2 oz (50 g) basmati rice until just soft, drain and mix with the other panful. Insert this mixture between the skin and flesh of the pheasant, cover with buttered paper, pour a little wine around and roast at Gas mark 8, 450°F (230°C) for 10 minutes, then reduce the temperature to Gas mark 6, 400°F (200°C) and cook for about 30–40 minutes. Any spare stuffing can be inserted into the chest cavity and spooned on to the plate when serving. The faint exotic aroma arising from the ginger gives a different dimension to this dish.

Lady Victoria Leatham

DOWN TO THE BONE

Pheasant, a luxury food in restaurants, can be deeply unpopular in private houses. Nobody at a dinner party wants to cope with lumps of meats, or worse still, bones. Casseroled pheasant, 'Vallée d'Auge' with cream, apple and celery, for instance, can be a delight, but it should not be merely jointed before serving – every scrap of meat should be stripped off the bones. This process does not take more than half an hour, even for two or three birds, after braising, and should be conducted by the non-cooking member of the household. He may discover that he can convert even the most jaded guest to a tolerance for pheasant.

Max Hastings
Editor-in-Chief, Daily Telegraph

SPEND MORE, EAT BETTER

If you're buying pheasants for the freezer, don't wait until January when they are cheap and plentiful. That is when they are old and tough. Better to pay more and be sure of a good meal when they are cooked – even in a casserole.

Christopher Leland
Farmer

THREE DAYS LATER

Marinate venison for three days in a liberal mixture of olive oil, any old wine, herbs and juniper berries before cooking it. Roast for 15 minutes to the pound in a double wrapping of foil spread with *masses* of butter and with some of the marinade spooned over. It never fails to be delicious.

Mrs Cherry Palmer

TO ROAST A SWAN

Take three pounds of Beef, beat fine in
a Mortar,

Put it into the swan – that is when
you've caught 'er

Then tie it up tight with a small piece
of tape

That the Gravy and other things may
not escape.

A Meal Paste (rather stiff) should be
laid on the Breast.

Some whitey-brown paper shall cover
the rest.

Fifteen minutes at least ere the Bird
you take down

Pull off the Paste that the breast may
get brown.

NB: The swan must *not* be skinned and a 15 lb
(7.5 kg) swan requires about two hours roasting,
with a fire not too fierce.

Mrs Benn Yeats-Brown

WAYS WITH VEGETABLES

*Then a sentimental passion of a vegetable fashion
must excite your languid spleen,
An attachment à la Plato for a bashful young potato,
or a not too French French bean.*

SIR W. S. GILBERT

MARINATED VEGETABLES

This attractive and different dish will serve four
people. Clean and cut into quarters a medium red,
yellow and green sweet pepper. Slice one green and
one yellow courgette and a medium aubergine. Trim
two Belgian endives and cut them in half. Fry all
these with 8 shiitake mushrooms, 4 red and 4 yellow
cherry tomatoes, 8 baby sweetcorn in 3 tablespoons
(45 ml) extra virgin olive oil. Season to taste and
mix ½ oz (15 g) of finely chopped rosemary and
thyme and 3 tablespoons (45 g) balsamic vinegar and
pour over the vegetables in the dish. Serve warm.

Anton Mosimann
Chef and Proprietor, Mosimann's, London

A LITTLE SEEDY

Every cookery book I've ever read tells you to remove the seeds from peppers before you do anything. While you don't want mouthfuls of them, the seeds have a nicely nutty, faintly peppery flavour which contributes to a good many dishes. So, don't work too hard to get rid of them, and even add a few to stuffings, salads or whatever.

Simone Sekers
Food writer

PEELING

If you need to peel a pepper – for ratatouille, say – pop it into a hot oven for a few minutes. Some people put it under the grill, but you have to watch it and turn it, so I prefer the oven method. Cover it whilst it cools so that the steam loosens the skin.

Lady Dashwood

… Peeling Jerusalem artichokes can be a fearfully fiddly business. Make it easier by bringing them to the boil in a pan of water and then blanching. The skins will peel away easily.

James Graham
Chef and Proprietor, Ostlers Close, Cupar

… Since peeling artichokes is such an awful job, try to inveigle someone else (perhaps your unsuspecting child) into doing it for you. And lemon juice will prevent this vegetable from discolouring and will counterbalance the artichoke's sweetness.

Raymond Blanc
*Chef and Proprietor,
Le Manoir aux Quat'Saisons, Great Milton*

FROZEN TOMATOES

Tomatoes can be frozen whole on trays, pips, skins,

calyx and all (the last imparts a fine scent to a tomato sauce), then tipped into polythene bags and added to stews in their frozen state.

Paul Levy
Food and wine writer, TV presenter

… I never bother to skin a tomato before freezing. When it comes out of the deep freeze and begins to defrost the skin just falls away.

Mrs Neil Petrie

TEARLESS

No need to wipe away the tears while peeling or chopping an onion: just leave the root on and you won't weep at all.

Laurie Meredith-Owens

… You won't cry when you peel onions if you sing, in tune, or not, as loudly as possible – a wonderful opportunity to give vent to any frustration you might feel as you prepare yet another meal.

Mrs Norman Hudson

… Always peel onions under water – that way you won't cry!

Bob Geldof
Pop star

… Take the tedium and the tears away from peeling button onions. Trim the root, plunge them into boiling water for 30 seconds, strain and put straight into cold water. Give them a squeeze and the onions will pop out of their skins.

Patrick McDonald
Chef and Proprietor, Epicurian, Cheltenham

QED

QUESTION: Why is one large onion better than two small ones?

ANSWER: One onion is quicker to peel than two.

Sir Clement Freud

QUICKER FRY

If you pour boiling water over sliced onions and then pat them dry they will fry much faster.

K. Finch

SALT FOR SEE-THROUGH EFFECT

Many recipes call for onions to be sweated so that they become transparent. Salt added to the frying pan will prevent them from sticking and burning and so the end result will be more satisfactory.

Erik Michel
Chef and Proprietor, Michels, Ripley

THINK BIG

Buy big bags of dried onion at the Cash and Carry and you will never need to peel and slice an onion again. As good as the real thing for everything with the exception of fried onions.

Mrs John Clark

TRUE GRIT

Leeks trimmed and cleaned in advance can be left, root ends upwards, in a jug or large glass of cold water. Any grit remaining should be drawn out by the time you come to cook them.

George Baker
Actor and cook

NOT AN OLD CHESTNUT

Buy chestnuts when they're young and shiny. Deep freeze them and when required, snip off the pointed end. Place on a baking tray and cook in a medium oven for 10–15 minutes, still frozen. Remove from the oven and place in a warmed casserole to retain heat. The shell and skin can then be removed with ease.

Jennifer Paterson
Food writer

GOLDEN PARSNIPS

Slice parsnips into rounds, boil and drain on to kitchen paper. Fry over a medium heat in a little butter with a sprinkling of caster sugar until golden brown on both sides.

Mary Whiting
Food writer and teacher

COLOURFUL

Boil equal quantities of carrots and swedes (preferably in a pressure cooker) and liquidize in a food processor with a little of the cooking liquid and butter for a distinguished and colourful purée to accompany any roast.

Derek Waring
Actor

BRIGHT GREENS

Always put a small lump of butter in the water when cooking any green vegetable – especially runner beans – and they will be a wonderfully bright green.

The Lady Fanshawe

43

GOODNESS

Steaming is an old art worth relearning. Steamed vegetables retain not only their flavour but also their health-giving vitamins.

Clare Francis
Author

GREENER GREENS

If you are not steaming, but boiling green vegetables, always put a pinch of bicarbonate of soda in the water. They come up greener than ever.

Diana Rigg
Actress

FRESH AND WHITE

Keep the smell of cabbage from spreading into every room by putting a slice of lemon in the cooking water.

Cauliflower will become beautifully white if you add a little milk to the cooking water.

Veronica Hubbard
Housekeeper

ABSORBENT

The smell of cauliflower cooking can invade the whole house. If you float a slice of bread on top of the water it will absorb the odours.

Lady Alliot

GREEN AND WHITE

Cauliflower and broccoli are often sold together nowadays. To make an attractive serving, cook them in the same pan and drain. Place alternately in a pudding basin, flowers to the outside, filling the middle with untidy bits. Keep warm until ready to turn out into a serving dish – a green and white mound.

Ann Miller
Manageress, Katharine House Hospice Shop, Bicester

AUBERGINE

I believe this is a personal discovery of a short cut. When you want to fry, grill or bake aubergines, don't bother to salt the cut pieces and leave them for half an hour so that the bitter juices drain away. Instead, simply drop them into a saucepan of boiling salted water for five minutes or so until just soft, adding a little lemon juice or white wine vinegar to the water to keep them pale. Then drain, pat really dry and cook again as you wish – they also cook more quickly, of course.

Josceline Dimbleby
Food writer

BE PREPARED

Vegetables can be 'blanched and refreshed', that is, prepared in advance in the morning for the evening. Place them in boiling water until they are on the point of being cooked, then drain and put immediately into cold water, ideally with ice in it. They can then be kept until required for the meal and reheated in boiling salted water for instant service.

Richard Smith
Chef and Proprietor, The Beetle and Wedge Hotel,
Moulsford-on-Thames

KEEPING WARM

If you need to keep drained vegetables or rice warm for a while before serving, keep them in the saucepan with several sheets of kitchen paper on the pan before putting on the lid. The paper absorbs the steam which does not then fall back to make the vegetable soggy.

Elisabeth Ray
Journalist

RELIEVING THE BOREDOM

I think courgettes are so boring that they need help. Boil them briskly but *briefly,* then take some of the water and combine it with a basic sauce which you have made with ½ oz (15 g) butter, ½ oz (15 g) of flour and ¼ pt (150 ml) single cream, and add *fresh* marjoram and nutmeg. The result is nicely herby and tarts up a desperately dull vegetable.

Colin McDowell
Author

CUCUMBER AND CREAM

Peel three large cucumbers and cut them into short sticks, removing all the seeds and leaving only firm flesh; set aside to drain in a sieve for as long as is convenient. Melt 1 oz (25 g) of butter in a large non-stick frying pan, tip in the cucumber sticks and fry until all moisture is driven off and the odd stick is turning brown. Pour on 10 fl oz (300 ml) of thick cream, add a handful of finely chopped mint, season with freshly ground pepper and salt. Bring to the boil, stirring well until the cream thickens and pour into a serving dish.

Mrs Maldwin Drummond

A PINCH OF SUGAR

A little sugar sprinkled on tomatoes before grilling them not only enhances the flavour but also speeds up the browning.

Ken Goody
Chef and Proprietor, The Cemlyn, Harlech

PEAS, PERFECT PEAS

The most satisfactory way I have found to cook frozen peas is to put them in a saucepan with a teaspoonful each of sugar and salt, a knob of butter and a sprig of mint. Cook over a low heat with the lid on and *no water*.

Mrs J. E. H. Collins

MIX AND MATCH

As a hostess one is always aware of presentation, and how food looks is very important. Frozen peas are now of such high quality that because of their conformity you can always tell that they've come from a packet. Now I mix the sizes. A petit pois packet with standard garden-sized ones achieves the irregularity of form and size of home-shelled ones. The result not only looks nicer but tastes better, I think.

The Lady Porchester

SUPER SPROUTS

Boil Brussels sprouts in vegetable stock or water until barely done. Drain. Toss for a minute in a little melted butter, lemon juice and freshly ground black pepper. The resulting tangyness hides the bitter flavour.

Mary Whiting
Food writer and teacher

DONE FOR THE BIG DAY

Brussels sprouts with the Christmas turkey are traditional in our house but we save time on Christmas Day by cooking and puréeing them some time before and freezing the purée in the dish in which it is to be served. Then it is just a matter of remembering to get the purée out of the freezer on Christmas Eve and heating it up with a good sprinkling of nutmeg on the day.

Richard Vanderpump

EARLY PEEL

It can often make life easier if you peel potatoes the day before you plan to cook them. If you put them, peeled, in a bowl of cold water with a slice of bread they won't go brown and slimy.

Mrs Cherry Palmer

… You can keep peeled potatoes white if you add a squeeze of lemon or a slice or two to the cold water in which they are waiting.

Mrs Gladys Humphrey

ROSEMARY POTATOES

This is a delicious and really Italian way of cooking potatoes. Peel and slice about 2 lb (1 kg) of small potatoes. Melt 2 oz (50 g) butter and 4 tablespoons of olive oil in a pan with fresh sprigs of rosemary and tip in the potatoes, raw. Turn them, over the heat, to get them good and hot, then put the lid on, turn the heat down and leave them until cooked. They are supposed to be a bit stuck together and not browned.

Lady Dashwood

GARLIC POTATOES

Each summer we organize an outing to the National Trust Fête Champêtre at Stourhead. Everyone brings something for the feast which has to be easily transportable and preferably eaten with fingers. My speciality is garlic potatoes. They are delicious cold, easy to eat and take a minimum of preparation time – unlike quiche.

Take about 4 lb (2 kg) of washed Jersey mids (leave the skins on), 6 garlic cloves crushed, ½ oz (15 g) butter or some olive oil, and put them into a lidded casserole, adding a sprinkling of sea salt. Place in the oven on a very low heat, Gas mark ¼, 225°F (110°C) for as long as possible – I usually put it in before I go to bed and they are ready by the time the smell of garlic wakes me up in the morning. Nothing more to do than to transfer them to a picnic bowl and get myself ready.

Francine Lawrence
Editor, Country Living

LESS FAT

The best way to avoid chips or sautéd potatoes from absorbing too much fat is to boil them for a few minutes in water. This first cooking stage provides a seal, protecting the starch from too much fat.

Roland Klein
Designer

HALF TIME

Halve the time it takes to roast potatoes: parboil them, scrape them with a fork, roll in seasoned flour and freeze. When required, roast them in hot oil straight from the freezer.

The Countess of Shelburne

HOT STUFF

When I was playing Cinderella in Norwich (the home of Colman's mustard) I picked up this tip which has changed my roast potatoes from run-of-the-mill-all-right to wonderful! Parboil as normal and whilst roughing up the edges by shaking in the pan, sprinkle dried mustard powder over the potatoes so that they are well covered. Roast in the oven for the requisite time. Apparently mustard loses its heat when cooked so the potatoes have a special, difficult to define but quite delicious flavour.

Annabel Croft
Tennis professional

INSTANT ROAST POTATOES

Did you know that you can freeze roast potatoes? I often make twice as many as I need. After I have rolled the surplus on kitchen paper I pop them in the freezer. And there is no need to defrost them; half an hour in a hot oven with a little fat will do the trick.

Mrs Charles Shepley-Cuthbert

MEALY TATTIES

If you want to make potatoes extra dry after they have been boiled, pour off the water and take them outside into the fresh air and shake them for about thirty seconds.

Alan Craigie
Chef and Proprietor, Creel Restaurant, Orkney

LUMPLESS

I'm not known for my cooking skills, but my mashed potato is perfection because I never squidge them with a masher. I always push them through a sieve – there's absolutely no possibility of a lump that way.

Helen Pease

ULTIMATE MASH

I am a lover of potatoes – particularly mashed, of which I am a connoisseur. I have found a way to make them *perfectly* so that they will wait happily, even until the next day, before being served. At the end of the mashing process (I use warmed milk, butter and an egg yolk, to taste) fold in a whipped egg white or two, using a metal spoon. Pop the mixture into a buttered ovenproof dish, dot with butter and make attractive fork patterns over the top. Heat it in the oven (Gas mark 6, 400°F (200°C)) half an hour before you want to eat. It saves so much last-minute fiddling.

Sue Lawley
TV presenter

KEEP YOUR COAT ON

For really tasty mashed potatoes, always boil the potatoes with their skins on, which will prevent them from absorbing water – or bake them in their jackets. Then peel them and mash in the normal way, adding cream, butter and seasoning as required.

Erik Michel
Chef and Proprietor, Michels, Ripley

HOT DISH

When draining potatoes or pasta place the bowl in which they are to be served under the colander so that the hot cooking water will warm the bowl.

Patricia Lousada
Food writer

CYCLED

If you have to prepare a lot of potatoes for baking for a large number of people, place them in the dishwasher on a short, cool programme – without detergent of course – and they will be beautifully washed, leaving you time to prepare other things.

Mrs C. Uprichard

THE RIGHT JACKET

Never cook jacket potatoes in aluminium foil. Give them a wash, and just before putting them on a tray into a hot oven, wet them, prick with a fork and lightly cover with salt. Cook for about an hour, depending on the size. Absolutely delicious, every time.

Shirley Eaton
Actress

SPEED UP

Speed up the baking of a jacket potato by pushing two skewers crosswise through the middle.

Fiona Fullerton
Actress

INSTANT JACKET POTATOES

Keep a supply of cold baked potatoes for quick suppers. Pop them into a hot oven for 10 minutes for perfect results.

Lindsay Bareham
Food writer

SCOURED

Use a wire pan-scourer to rub the skins off new potatoes.

Mrs C. Edwards

A GOOD SOAKING

Before cooking new potatoes, prick them gently with a fork and soak them in water with plenty of salt and sugar for an hour; use the same water for boiling.

Ken Goody
Chef and Proprietor, The Cemlyn, Harlech

READY FOR SALAD

Potatoes in a potato salad should never be peeled because that is the way to lose the correct texture as well as the flavour. Boil the potatoes whole and when they are cool slip the skins off with your fingers. Now you have a peeled spud with the texture to absorb the flavours from the salad.

Colin McDowell
Author

NON-ABSORBENT

In order to prevent the potatoes in a potato salad from absorbing too much oil, add a soupspoonful of white wine to the dressing.

Roland Klein
Designer

REVIVAL COURSE

To revive lettuce, put it in a bowl that is almost too small for it, add about 1 in (2.5 cm) of water and leave in the fridge for an hour or two. The lettuce might be too far gone but you might as well try it.

Katharine Whitehorn
Journalist

TOMATO SALAD

Slice very ripe tomatoes with their skins on, arrange in a bowl and sprinkle lightly with caster sugar, ground black pepper, salt and chopped basil. Pour a little really good olive oil over them and eat about one hour later.

Marchioness of Tavistock

EVEN CRISPER

For a fresher salad, tear the salad leaves into pieces about half the size of a postcard. Never cut a lettuce – that allows all the liquid to drain out and you are left with a soft and floppy salad. As you tear the leaves, you crush the veins closed and the liquid is trapped in. Wash the pieces thoroughly, put in a clean tea-towel to dry – whirl it round your head if you like – until all the water has gone. Half an hour in the fridge after this will make it even crisper.

Michael Barry
TV cookery expert and food writer

LEST WE FORGET

Don't forget salads; served as a main course, starter or accompaniment, they are nutritious, colourful, refreshing, and usually quick and easy to prepare.

Christina Foyle
Director, Foyle's Bookshop

A MEAL IN ITSELF

This salad is our standard summer lunch. One tin of red kidney beans or chick peas, with, in whatever quantities you wish, chopped broccoli, avocado, mushrooms, tomato and crushed garlic if you don't mind breathing it over everyone. Toss in a vinaigrette dressing.

Chris Bonington
Mountaineer

QUICK MIX

For an unusual and sustaining salad, toss watercress, walnuts and chunks of Gorgonzola with balsamic vinegar.

Lucy Gutteridge
Actress

INSTANT RIPENING

If an avocado isn't quite ripe enough for immediate consumption, cut it in half and experiment with a few seconds in the microwave on defrost setting. Alternatively, cover the exposed flesh with a good layer of butter or margarine, place it in a brown paper bag and keep it in a warm place for a while.

Mrs Steve Race

… Avocados ripen much more quickly if they are put into a large polythene bag with a banana. All fruit give off an odourless gas which is a ripening agent, and bananas give off more than most.

Lady Martha Ponsonby

BLACK OUT

When making avocado dips or guacamole, leave the avocado stone in the middle of the mixture. This prevents the concoction from turning black.

Lord Menuhin

RICE, PASTA AND PULSES

Eat slowly: only men in rags
And gluttons old as sin
Mistake themselves for carpet bags
And tumble victuals in.

SIR WALTER RALEIGH

AT HER MOTHER'S KNEE

My Burmese mother makes perfect rice and this is how she does it. Take a handful of basmati rice per person (don't bother to sieve and wash it three times – the supermarket stuff has already had that done to it). Put, say, eight handfuls in a medium-size saucepan with a very close-fitting lid, add water up to two knuckles from the top of the rice; in other words, stick a finger on the top of the rice and add water up to the second knuckle – it doesn't matter how big your hands are, it always works. Bring the rice to the boil without the lid and as soon as it has boiled turn it down to the very, very lowest heat, put the lid on and forget it for about twenty minutes. Then, when you remember it, there shouldn't be any moisture and the rice should be dry and crumbly.

Sue Arnold
Food writer, The Observer

RIGHT ABOUT RICE

I remember being very impressed when I was young by one of my teenage friends announcing that plain white rice took exactly 13 minutes to cook from the moment it was put into boiling water: she was right! Rinsing it in cold water afterwards stops it sticking, particularly if you want to reheat it.

Lady Morse

KEEP IT FLUFFY

Cooked rice will keep dry, fluffy and hot if, when you have boiled it and rinsed it well, you fluff it up in the colander, and put it over a pan of hot water with a teacloth over the top. It will happily wait for hours like this.

Mrs Gerhard Bülle

AS IF BY MAGIC

I find my method with rice a boon when entertaining. I boil it in the normal way and rinse it in a wire strainer under the cold tap for about five minutes when it is cooked. Then I leave it to drain for an hour or so. When the moment comes for it to be served I pop it in the microwave for three minutes, stir it twice and there is perfect fluffy rice as if by magic.

Victor Spinetti
Actor

GET AHEAD

Rice is best for stir-frying if it has been cooked at least six hours earlier.

Annie Morley-Slim
Cookery teacher, Westminster Adult Education Service

SO SIMPLE

This is a really simple but delicious risotto. Just boil the rice in the usual way, strain it and heat it up with extra virgin olive oil, a little lemon juice, garlic pickle and a *lot* of pesto.

Iris Murdoch
Author

FOOLPROOF COUSCOUS

Cooking couscous for a large number of people doesn't have to be a problem. The art lies in keeping the grain separate and fluffy and not letting it stick in lumps. I put the couscous in a huge clay dish that will go in the oven, adding warm salted water – a bit less than the volume of the couscous – and stir very well so that it is absorbed evenly. After about 15 minutes I add about 3 tablespoons of sunflower oil to every pound of couscous and rub the grain between my hands. About 20 minutes before I am ready to serve I put the dish in a hot oven covered with aluminium foil.

Claudia Roden
Food writer

THE GREEKS HAD A WORD FOR IT

The ancient Greeks ate a lot of beans but were, not surprisingly, worried by the flatulence they incurred. Their answer to the problem was in the cooking and Dioscorides's advice in the first century AD is the same as mine today. Whenever cooking beans or pulses of any kind, including lentils, bring them to the boil, cook for three minutes and strain, discarding the water. Start again with fresh water.

If you are cooking black-eyed beans and would like them to stay a nice colour rather than go murky, once you have strained them and added fresh water also add a couple of tablespoons of fresh lemon juice. Greek wisdom at its most fundamental.

Rena Salaman
Food writer

A GOOD SOAK

When using dried mushrooms for pasta dishes or risottos, place them in a bowl and cover them with sherry rather than water. Leave them to stand until soft before using. The soaking liquid itself can be strained and used to give added flavour to the finished dish.

Anna Best, Peta Brown and Jane Barker
Instructors, Young Cooks of Britain

PERFECT PASTA

I discovered this method for cooking hard pasta on the back of a pasta packet in Clapham in 1974 and have used it ever since. Put a large saucepan of water on to boil and add a pinch of salt and a little olive oil. When it is boiling put the pasta in and boil it for three minutes. Take it off the heat, put the lid on and leave it for seven minutes. At the end of that time it will be perfectly cooked, not sticky but perfectly *al dente*.

Michael Barry
TV cookery expert and food writer

NON-STICK PASTA

A little olive oil added to the water in which pasta is cooked will prevent it from sticking together.

Robert Lyons
Resident Director, The Bay Horse Inn, Ulverston

NEAPOLITAN TRICK

When you have cooked pasta, drain the water into another container, then ladle some of this liquid over the spaghetti, tagliatelle or whatever, until it has 'drunk' it. This will prevent the pasta from ever sticking together. It's an old Neapolitan trick which has never failed me.

Katie Boyle
TV personality

MELLOW YELLOW

A wonderful Italian cook once told me that when making fresh pasta, it helps to add a pinch of saffron to the dough – eggs in this country just aren't yellow enough. Ever since, I've followed her advice and it works a treat.

Rachel Cooke
Food writer, The Sunday Times

HERB PASTA

You can save time when you're making herb-flavoured fresh pasta by whirling the desired herbs in the blender with the eggs before adding the flour, saving on all that laborious chopping.

Roger Pergl-Wilson
Chef and Proprietor, Rogers, Windermere

NON-STICK NOODLES

After cooking enough dried noodles for two

people in boiling water, plunge them into cold water, strain and add 1 teaspoon soya sauce and half a tablespoon of sesame oil. This helps to prevent the noodles from sticking together.

Siew Choo Calthorpe
Cookery teacher, Westminster Adult Education Service

PASTA STYLE

Eating pasta properly is an art. When it arrives at the table on the plate it must be loosened so that every string is evenly coated with sauce. Then push the pasta to the side to make a space where a few strings at a time can be masterfully turned around the fork to create a mouthful neither too large nor too small. Only when the forkful is tidied and collated should it be transferred to the mouth.

Antonio Carluccio
Chef and Proprietor, The Neal Street Restaurant, London

FLAVOURS, HERBS AND GARNISHES

Nose, nose, jolly red nose,
Who gave me this jolly red nose?
Nutmegs and ginger, cinnamon and cloves
And they gave me this jolly red nose.

JOHN FLETCHER

THE BIG BUILD-UP

When seasoning a dish, always start with salt to establish the base, then, to build up layers and length of taste, add spices. Lastly add acid – vinegar, lemon juice, etc.

Raymond Blanc
Chef and Proprietor, Le Manoir aux Quat'Saisons,
Great Milton

BALANCE

Salt balance is a key to all savoury food and while it can be added, it can never be taken away. While cooking, taste, taste, then taste again, but never forget that a teaspoon here and another there is a different experience from eating a full portion where dominant salt is wholly destructive.

Richard Whittington
Writer and cook

FINGERS OUT

Never use your finger to test for seasoning. It's a question not of hygiene but of practicality. Use a large spoon to test soup and a teaspoon to test a sauce. What tastes fine in a small quantity isn't necessarily good by the bowlful and vice versa.

Shaun Hill
Head Chef, Gidleigh Park, Chagford

CORRECTION

I made this discovery when cooking for my husband, who was a stickler for savoury dishes being well-seasoned. If you can't quite get it right, try a few drops of cider vinegar. It seems to balance all the flavours in the most marvellous way, particularly in soups and stews.

Mrs C. A. Weatherby

IT'S THE ESSENCE

Anchovy essence gives a lift to so many dishes. Shepherd's pie with at least a teaspoonful (I use more) and a handful of thyme is transformed. Fish pies and salad niçoise both benefit from liberal sprinklings.

Mrs John Biffen

SHOPPING BASKET

Go to the chemist for oil of peppermint (for making peppermint creams etc.), almond oil for salted almonds, glycerine to stop icing turning to rock and eye-droppers for measuring tiny amounts.

Mary Goldring
Freelance economist

SECRETS

There are three secret ingredients I always keep. First, dried mushrooms (Boletus) – the *cèps* of France or the *porcini* of Italy – which add wonderful flavours to stocks, fillings, stews or sauces. Then a tube of harissa, the North African chilli and spice paste, to add a little 'umph' to many dishes. And third, a tube of anchovy paste to lighten flavours, as the Romans did with their *garum* and South East Asians do with *nam pla* fish sauce. And of course, good olive oil is the greatest non-secret ingredient.

Nicola Cox
Cookery writer and demonstrator

HOT FAVOURITE

I normally hate tuna fish, but it's such a popular sandwich filling that I've stolen the New Yorker idea of mixing it with a little horseradish. Unlikely? Surprising! And very more-ish.

Jane Lapotaire
Actress

DIP

Powdered mustard added to Hellmann's mayonnaise makes a wonderful dip for sausages. Use 1 teaspoon of mustard powder to each 2 tablespoons of mayonnaise. Don't make it too far ahead of time, though, as it tends to go runny.

Mrs Roddy Llewellyn

A SPOONFUL OF SUGAR

Tomato purée tastes much better in dishes if you add a little caster sugar to it.

Lady Morse

HELD AT BAY

Three bay leaves added to the water in which a bacon joint is boiling will greatly enhance the flavour.

Dora Saint ('Miss Read')
Author

ENHANCEMENT

When making a savoury mousseline with, say, chicken or fish, reduce some appropriate stock until it is syrupy and add it to the mousse whilst beating in the cream. This will replace the flavour of the meat or fish purée which is diluted by the addition of the cream.

Allan Holland
Head Chef, Mallory Court, Leamington Spa

RETURN TO BLENDER

You will get bread sauce that actually tastes of something if, when you have flavoured the milk with a clove-studded onion, you take the cloves out of the onion (making sure it is properly cooked) and put it in the blender with a little more milk. Return this to the pan for a little longer on a very low gas.

Katharine Whitehorn
Journalist

A HINT OF CHEESE

On a recent cookery visit to Italy we were introduced to the idea of adding the rind of Parmesan cheese to a fish or meat stock for the last hour of cooking – it really is a great flavour enhancer.

The Lady Brocket

SAUCE OF INSPIRATION

Instead of always adding wines etc. to your sauces, you can achieve surprising results by whisking vinaigrettes in at the last minute. For example, to enhance a good chicken sauce, whisk in an olive oil and sherry dressing; or in the case of a duck sauce, a raspberry vinaigrette goes well. The combinations and flavours to be discovered are immense and it's good fun inventing new sauces.

Steven Blake
Executive Head Chef, The Royal Crescent Hotel, Bath

SAVOY SAUCE

If you would like a sauce full of flavour and goodness, but haven't time to stand in the kitchen all day, follow this recipe:

Chop 1 lb (450 g) chicken carcasses and bones into the smallest possible pieces and roast in a hot oven with 3 tablespoons of oil for 10 minutes. Meanwhile, chop 2 onions, 2 carrots, 1 leek and 1 celery stalk and add them to the chicken bones and cook for another ten minutes or until the bones are browned. Coarsely chop 2 tomatoes and add to the mixture with 3 oz (80 g) of tomato paste, 2 peeled garlic cloves, a bay leaf and a sprig of thyme. Stir well and cook for ten more minutes. Pour the mixture into a stockpot and boil 10 fl oz (300 ml) of wine in the roasting pan, stirring well to dissolve all the browned bits. Add this to the stockpot, stir well, and bring to the boil. Add 4 pt (2.25 litres) of chicken stock, bring to the boil again and simmer until reduced by half, skimming occasionally.

Strain, and freeze in small quantities. This is a perfect basic sauce.

Anton Edelmann
Maître Chef des Cuisines, The Savoy, London

WITH A PINCH OF SALT

A pinch of salt added to mustard when you're making a new pot works wonders: it keeps it from going hard for much longer.

Lady Connell

TASTE THAT TANG

Before you peel an orange, get out your swivel-blade potato peeler and thinly slice away the zest. Drop the slivers into any stews to give a tangy, zesty flavour. You can dry the zest (resting on a piece of kitchen foil) in the airing cupboard or the switched off oven after you have cooked a roast and store it in an air-tight jar – it will keep for ages.

Dorothy Tutin
Actress

HERBAL VERSATILITY

Do you know a lovely herb called salad burnet? The flowers look like bees; the leaves, if sprinkled on a salad will give it a *je ne sais quoi* and substitute very well for cucumbers.

Baroness Trumpington
Baroness-in-waiting, House of Lords

FLOWERY

When you buy parsley, cut off the bottom of the stalks – just as you would flowers – and put the parsley in a glass of water. It will keep for up to two weeks this way.

Jan Leeming
TV presenter

CHOP CHOP

This is a way to avoid chopping parsley. Put it in a plastic bag and put it in the freezer. When you want to use it, open the end of the bag and bash the parsley with a rolling pin. Allow it to defrost and squeeze it dry. It will be as if finely chopped.

Kevin Mangeolles
Head Chef, Michaels Nook, Grasmere

QUICK SNIP

I always put parsley in a cup and snip it with scissors. Much easier than with a knife on a board and works with other herbs too.

Mrs Neil Kinnock

… My mother's old black cook taught me that there is a technique to chopping parsley – or any herb – on a board. Take a sharp knife with a slightly convex blade and, holding the tip of the knife firmly in one place on the board, chop, moving in a semi-circle backwards and forwards over the herbs. Scoop together once or twice, repeating the chopping. It's all over in moments.

Mrs Constantine Sidamon-Eristoff

TWICE AS GOOD

When using parsley in any recipe, chop the leaves and then blanch them for ten seconds. This will double the flavour.

Bruno Loubet
Chef and Proprietor, Bistro Bruno, London

SAVING THYME

We have a variety of thyme bushes in our garden and enjoy the flavours in casseroles, stuffings and soups. However, removing the leaves from the stalks is a very fiddly job. We get over this by placing the herb in a plastic bag and freezing it. On taking it out of the freezer one can shake and rub the thyme vigorously whilst it is still in the bag – the leaves will now be separated from the stalks. This method works equally well with other herbs, particularly rosemary and marjoram.

Christopher and Joanna Wickens
Proprietors, Wickens, Northleach

BOX CLEVER

I always prefer to pick fresh herbs all the year round but it requires care and attention to enjoy basil, coriander, dill and even parsley all year. I pick sprigs of these herbs and trim them to the length of a lidded plastic box. Freeze them and break off when needed. No good for salads but superb for cooking and the stems give added flavour.

Caroline Holmes
Lecturer and demonstrator, Gourmet Gardening

HERBAL CRUMBLE

When you have a quantity of fresh herbs, dry them in the microwave oven, crumble them and store in an air-tight jar.

Anne Nicholls
Cookery Consultant and Principal,
Bonne Bouche School of Cookery

REVIVAL

You can make dried herbs taste fresh if you chop an equal amount of parsley into them. It's the moisture and the chlorophyll that do the trick.

Head Brownell

CUBIC

When I freeze basil I whirl it in the whizzer with a little water, put it into ice-cube trays, and when it is frozen I shake the cubes into polythene bags to store.

Susan Hampshire
Actress

HEY PESTO

Got a glut of fresh basil in the summer? Make pesto, a paste of basil, garlic, pine nuts and olive oil – a good cook book will give the recipe – which will store for a few months in an air-tight jar in the fridge. And don't throw away the stems: put them in oil to flavour vinaigrettes.

James Graham
Chef and Proprietor, Ostlers Close, Cupar

... I make my pesto by processing 2 cups of fresh basil leaves, 4 cloves of garlic and 1 cup of walnut pieces. Don't overdo the processing – it's nicer crunchy. With the machine still running, pour in 1 cup of good olive oil. Stop the machine, add 1 cup of freshly grated Parmesan cheese and seasoning, and give it a final whirl.

Mrs Richard Burton

ANOTHER WAY

Basil is often recommended for sprinkling on tomatoes; I think it is delicious on buttered carrots. Try it and see.

Alan Titchmarsh
Gardener and broadcaster

VERSATILE GINGER

Here are three ways with root ginger:

Peel it with a potato peeler and then grate it on the fine holes of a hand-grater.

Keep slices of ginger in a small jar of sherry. It is then preserved and the flavoured sherry is excellent for a Chinese stir-fry.

Fried shreds of ginger – sizzled for a minute in a tiny pan of butter or oil – are good to scatter over fancy salads and go well with scallops and prawns.

Lynda Brown
Food writer

… When I peel fresh ginger roots I score the skin in several places, pour boiling water over and leave until the skin starts to lift (30 seconds or so). I then run the roots under cold water and ease the skin off with a sharp knife.

Caroline Holmes
Lecturer and writer, Gourmet Gardening

JUST A HINT

To enhance the flavour of stir-fried meat or poultry, fry a thumb-sized piece of peeled root ginger in the oil until it browns, discarding the ginger before stir-frying.

Siew Choo Calthorpe
Cookery teacher, *Westminster Adult Education Service*

HINT, HINT

If just a hint of garlic is required, rub the clove around the cooking vessel instead of actually putting it in with the other ingredients.

Germain Schwab
Patron, Winteringham Fields, South Humberside

IF PRESSED

If you are using a garlic press to crush garlic, don't bother to peel the garlic first. The papery skin remains behind in the press as the garlic is squeezed through. No more smelly fingers.

Catherine Blakeley
Catherine Blakeley's Cookery Courses, Newport

BRING OUT THE MOISTURE

Sprinkle salt on garlic while chopping it. This brings out the moisture and makes chopping it finely a lot easier.

Marc Preston
Head Chef, La Fleur de Lys Restaurant, Shaftesbury

OLD-FASHIONED

I find the traditional pestle and mortar much the quickest and most efficient tool to use for crushing garlic. And separate the cloves by bashing the stalk end of the bulb down on to your work surface.

The Lady Wardington

EASY PEEL

The easy way to peel garlic cloves is to drop them into a pan of boiling water for thirty seconds, drain, refresh under cold water and slip the skins off with your fingers.

Patricia Lousada
Food writer

… Microwave garlic cloves for a few seconds before peeling to make them easier to peel. To get rid of the smell on your hands, rub them with a lemon before washing.

Lady Cazalet

A COLD WASH

Always wash your hands in cold water after dealing with garlic or onions. Hot water seals in the smell. (A friend who is a very good cook didn't know this, so if she didn't I'm assuming others don't either.)

Jan Leeming
TV presenter

STRONG AND FRESH

Crushed garlic has a stronger flavour than sliced or chopped. And to prevent the lingering smell or taste of garlic in the mouth, chew fresh parsley after the meal.

HRH The Duchess of York

ROAST GARLICS

Whole garlic bulbs can be roasted in about ½ inch (1.25 cm) of stock for about 30 minutes. If the stalk has been trimmed to just below the top of the clove it can then be pressed with a fork to release the purée – delicious with lamb.

Jean Alexander
Catering Manager, Forest Mere, Liphook

NOT DEAD, BUT BURIED

Garlic which has sprouted is stale and acrid, way past its best for cooking. But don't throw it away. Plant the cloves just under the soil, in a window box if you haven't got a garden, and snip at the long green shoots, as you would with chives, to flavour omelettes, stews, etc.

Lynda Brown
Food writer

73

EVER READY

Here's a way to have fresh garlic always to hand and wonderful garlic-flavoured oil ready for frying onions or making soups etc. Skin some garlic cloves, crush them and then place in a food processor (or chop them) until not quite a purée. Put in a screw-topped jar and pour in olive oil to about 2 in (5 cm) above the garlic.

Irene Reeve
Chef and Proprietor, The Old Vicarage, Witherslack

… You can do much the same with fresh red chillies, pricking them before submerging them in the oil, which you can then use sparingly when 'heat' is required.

Ken Goody
Chef and Proprietor, The Cemlyn, Harlech

TOO HOT TO HANDLE

The smaller the chilli, the hotter it will be. Take care when handling. Before you cut one to get rid of the seeds (the hottest part) rub your hands with plenty of fine salt; this counteracts the heat. Wash your hands immediately after handling the chilli before touching anything. And if you accidentally bite into a hot chilli and can't bear it, eat a few mouthfuls of plain boiled rice or a piece of cucumber. Cold water and chilled lager, sadly, have very little effect.

Sri Owen
Food writer

DAISY, DAISY

The chef who used to work at Burghley in the

1960s had a very tiny set of metal cutters in different shapes that he used for preparing garnishes. You can still get them at specialist cookery shops. He would slice a stuffed olive, then with the help of the flower-shaped cutter, would make it look like a daisy. Very thin strips of cucumber skin made 'leaves' and although simple this was one of the most attractive garnishes when applied to any jellied surface such as a cold salmon or mousse.

Lady Victoria Leatham

RED ALERT

Put slices of beetroot in melted redcurrant jelly and leave to set. Appetizing to look at and delicious with cold meat.

Lady Cazalet

FRIED GARNISH

Deep-fry the leaves of fresh herbs such as flat-leaf parsley, lovage and basil to make a lovely garnish for fish dishes or the top of a salad.

David Wilson
Chef and Proprietor, The Peat Inn, Cupar

TAKE ME HIGH

It is important to make dishes look fresh and exciting. I do this by creating as much height as possible with every piece of garnish.

Adam Palmer
Head Chef, Champneys, Tring

SAY IT WITH FLOWERS

Flowers and herbs are my favourite form of garnish. Small sprays of coriander or flat-leaf parsley can be arched over grilled fish or meat; nasturtium, borage or pansy flowers can be tossed into salads; while a pudding can be transformed with a scattering of rose petals, primroses or violets.

Sybil Kapoor
Food writer

... Decorate the top of an egg mousse with nasturtium flowers: they are pretty to look at and the peppery flavour adds interest.

Penelope Hughes-Hallett

SAUCES AND SALAD DRESSINGS

Every course needs a good sauce.

ELIZA COOPER

PERFECT WHITE SAUCE

Many years ago a French friend told me that the British fussed far too much in the making of béchamel sauce. 'Gently and slowly pour the already warmed milk on to a roux and carefully stir for some minutes.' *Nonsense!* Melt the butter, stir in the flour, turn up the heat and pour in cold milk quickly. Stir for about 30 seconds *et voilà!* Perfect white sauce.

Rosalie Crutchley
Actress

DOUBLE UP

If you are making either bread or apple sauce, use a double saucepan. You simply put the ingredients into the top pan, water in the bottom one and leave on the stove (but don't let the water boil away). The sauces will cook without stirring; you simply mash the contents with a fork before serving it and you won't have a sticky pan to soak and clean.

Elizabeth Jane Howard
Author

LUMPLESS

I learnt this when I was a bachelor and it has stood me in good stead ever since. If you get lumps in your gravy or white sauce don't waste time trying to smooth them out with your wooden spoon. Whack the whole lot into the food processor and whizz it up. Pour it back into the pan to re-heat – a perfect result every time.

Julian Fellowes
Actor

SKINLESS

To avoid getting a skin on top of a white sauce-in-waiting make it as usual but use only two thirds of the milk. Remove from the heat and pour the remaining milk carefully over the top and leave, without stirring, until the time has come to dish up. Then reheat, stirring well and the sauce will be perfect.

HRH The Duchess of York

… After making a sauce or custard, wring out some greaseproof paper in water and place it firmly over the hot sauce. A little may stick to the paper when you remove it but it will prevent a skin from forming.

Incidentally, Lakelands Plastics, who are very good for all kitchen equipment, produce a long roll of greaseproof paper cut to the perfect width for circling a soufflé dish – and one roll lasts for ages.

Mrs Cherry Palmer

… When I want to stop a sauce from forming a skin I cover it with a thin plastic bag – the sort that fish or meat are now put in at the supermarket. Be careful, though, if the pan is very hot lest the bag melts against it.

The Lady Hesketh

SHINE

A knob of butter whisked into a béchamel sauce at the last minute will give it a gloss.

Thr Hon. Mrs Petrie

LAZY COOK

When I'm feeling lazy (most of the time) I flavour the milk for bread sauce with a handful of dried onion and cloves. No one has complained yet.

The Lady Wardington

ONION SKINS

When you are boiling up a chicken carcass for stock with onion, herbs, etc., *do not peel the onion*. The stock will be just as flavoursome and the onion skin will give it a lovely rich colour, much more appetizing than the usual pallid grey. Not peeling the onion saves time and tears too, so there's an added bonus.

Victoria Glendinning
Journalist

BEATING TIME

This is my sure-fire way to make a mayonnaise without fear of it curdling. Using the ingredients of your usual recipe, beat two egg yolks with 1 teaspoon of powdered mustard and a teaspoon of vinegar for *five minutes* with a balloon whisk or *three minutes* with an electric beater, then pour the oil in, about 10 fl oz (300 ml), whisking all the time. If you patiently beat the egg yolks for the above time it doesn't matter how quickly you add the oil.

Lady Willoughby de Broke

TEN-SECOND MAYONNAISE

To make mayonnaise in 10 seconds, put the whole egg, seasoning, 1 tablespoon of lemon juice or vinegar into a liquidizer, switch on and pour 5 fl oz (150 ml) oil gently through the top on to the whirling mixture. All done.

Mrs Margaret Dunker

MOTHER'S RUIN

A drop of gin in the mayonnaise works wonders with seafood. (A drop of gin in the cook works even better.)

Elisabeth Luard
Cookery columnist, The Scotsman

TAKE THE TEMPERATURE

It is my belief that mayonnaise is more likely to curdle if it is made with eggs straight out of the fridge and oil out of a warm cupboard.

The Lady Wardington

ICE-CUBE CURE

Should mayonnaise start to curdle when you are making it by hand, drop an ice-cube into the mixture (or one teaspoon of very cold water) and whisk like mad. Gradually the luscious, creamy texture will be restored.

Sue Lawrence
Food writer

BLENDER HOLLANDAISE

Hollandaise sauce is made in a moment by this foolproof method: place 1 tablespoon tarragon vinegar and 2 tablespoons lemon juice in one saucepan and 6 oz (175 g) butter in another; heat them both until the vinegar and lemon juice are bubbling and the butter melted without burning.

In the blender mix 3 egg yolks and 1 teaspoon caster sugar (just enough to break up the yolks and incorporate the sugar). Add the boiling vinegar and juice slowly whilst the blender is running and then add the melted butter, still whirling. Season with a little salt and paprika to taste. The sauce will keep for several hours in a bain-marie (but never boil the water).

Peter Wilson
Chef and Proprietor, Langley House Hotel, Wiveliscombe

KEEPING IT WARM

You can save some of those precious last minutes when dishing up a meal if you make hollandaise sauce in advance and keep it in a wide-topped thermos flask, previously warmed with hot water.

Michael Mander

LEFT-OVERS

Three uses for left-over hollandaise, béarnaise, sauce beurre blanc, etc.:

1. Mix ½ cup of sauce with a cup of mashed potato and two cups of flaked fish to make perfect fishcakes.

2. For a brown top to a gratin, dot with left-over sauce and put under the grill or bake in the oven.

3. Add to mashed potato – delicious.

Myrtle Allen
Chef and Proprietor, Ballymaloe House, County Cork

SMASH HIT

Sprinkle a pinch of Smash in any sauces prone to curdle and it will avert disasters.

Countess Michaelowska

HEALING THE SPLIT

This tip should restore even the worst split sauces. Boil a little cream in the bottom of a deep, narrow pan. *Slowly* pour in the *hot* split sauce and whizz with an electric hand-held beater until completely smooth again.

Nick Nairn
Chef and Proprietor, Braeval Old Mill, Stirling

TO THE RESCUE

It is possible to save a hollandaise or béarnaise sauce when it curdles. Either beat an egg yolk in a small bowl and then beat in some of the curdled mixture, return to the curdled sauce and gently mix. Or, if you have run out of eggs, boil some water. Put a tablespoon of boiled water into a small, warmed bowl and continue as above.

Pamela, Lady Harlech

SAVED

Béarnaise sauce can suddenly curdle as you bring it to the table. Don't panic. Take it back to the kitchen, and pour the sauce into a large bowl on to four ice-cubes. Stir very quickly and fish out the ice, wiping the sauce off with your fingers. Dash back to the table and serve the now cooler but no longer curdled sauce.

The Lady May

TOGETHERNESS

Egg and cream liaisons can be tricky and prone to curdle. Just a teaspoonful of arrowroot mixed with a drop or two of milk added to the mixture should keep it on the straight and narrow.

Mrs Kenneth Harper

THREE FINGERS

Fill a jam-jar with one finger of wine vinegar, plus two fingers of olive oil. Add the usual herbs and seasoning and shake. Perfect vinaigrette every time and it's made in a moment.

Mrs Alan Tritton

HOT STUFF

Add a pinch of curry powder to your customary French dressing and it will taste as if you have used walnut oil.

Countess Michaelowska

ABOVE ITS STATION

As an impoverished student I learned to store olives in a jar of unflavoured oil. The oil mellows the flavour of the olives and in exchange the olives impart enough pungency to the oil to elevate it above its station as a salad dressing.

Rosemary Stark
Food writer

QUICK CHANGE

For a quick salad dressing try using one of the flavoured oils now available in many shops and supermarkets.

Anna Best, Peta Brown and Jane Barker
Instructors, Young Cooks Of Britain

IN THE DARK

Olive oil should always be kept in a cool, dark place. Sunlight causes oxidization which will eventually make it go rancid, so never buy a bottle which has been in the shop window or kept under bright lights. Ask for one which has been in store.

Lynda Brown
Food writer

FRUIT-FLAVOURED

Fruit vinegars are excellent bases for dressings and you can make your own during the soft fruit season. Raspberries, blackberries and strawberries all make good bases. Simply cover your chosen fruit with a good wine vinegar in an air-tight container. Leave this on the windowsill and in a couple of weeks the flavours will have married.

Christopher and Joanna Wickens
Proprietors, Wickens, Northleach

ZING

Instead of adding mustard, an incredibly easy way to put a bit of zing into an otherwise boring vinaigrette is to add a generous teaspoon of pesto and shake well: it gives a fresh spicy flavour to any salad.

Loyd Grossman
Food writer and television presenter

SWEETY

Ignore the purists and add a teaspoonful of caster sugar when making mayonnaise or French dressing.

Ken Goody
Chef and Proprietor, The Cemlyn, Harlech

GINGER IT UP

As the summer wears on and you become bored with your usual salad dressing, you can liven it up considerably with the following: make the dressing in your normal way but add a small pinch of *freshly* ground ginger to the mixture before shaking it up.

Colin McDowell
Author

DRESSED UP

We keep our salad dressing in a small wine decanter with a well-fitting glass stopper (so that it doesn't leak when we shake it up). It looks quite attractive on the dining table.

The Lady Wardington

VERSATILE TRIO

We suggest three light and different dips which take moments to make and are very low in calories:

- 3 tablespoons low-calorie mayonnaise mixed with 1 tablespoon horseradish sauce.
- 3 tablespoons Greek yoghurt mixed with 1½ tablespoons mango chutney.
- 2 tablespoons low-calorie mayonnaise mixed with 1 tablespoon cranberry sauce and 1 tablespoon freshly squeezed orange juice.

Paul Spink
Head Chef, Ragdale Hall, Melton Mowbray

DESSERTS AND FRUIT

What is the matter with Mary Jane?
She's perfectly well and she hasn't a pain
She's crying with all her might and main
And it's lovely rice pudding for dinner again.

A. A. MILNE

ALL THINGS SPICE

The ingredients make this biscuit-based flan sound rather yukky but – trust me – the result is sharp, light and delicious. First line a 7-in (17.5 cm) pie plate with 8 oz (225 g) finely crushed ginger-nut biscuits, blended with 4 oz (100 g) melted butter. (Press the mixture flat with the back of a metal spoon.) Then lightly whip 5 fl oz (150 ml) double cream and fold in a small can of sweetened condensed milk, 6 tablespoons of fresh lemon juice and plenty of grated lemon rind. As soon as it starts to thicken, pour it into the biscuit case and chill as long as possible – preferably overnight.

Laurie Purden
Journalist

ROLL OVER PAVLOVA

Take a new look at that old friend from down-under, the pavlova. Line a swiss-roll tin with buttered foil, make your usual pavlova mixture (egg whites, sugar and a dash of vinegar) and smooth it into the tin. Bake in a medium oven, Gas mark 4, 350°F (180°C) for 20 minutes and while it is cooling, sprinkle caster sugar on to a clean tea-towel. Turn the pavlova/swiss-roll on to the sugared cloth, spread with whipped cream and dot with raspberries or strawberries. Roll it up and amaze your guests.

Mrs Neil Petrie

RULE OF THREE

Three tricks for perfect meringues: first, add a pinch of cream of tartar to the whites. Second, don't use a machine, always use a big balloon whisk. And third, put the sugar in the oven to dry out before sieving it into the whites.

Jack Straw MP

JAM SOUFFLÉ

This apricot soufflé takes only moments to prepare. Beat 4 egg yolks with 4 tablespoons of apricot jam. Whisk 4 egg whites and fold them into the yolk mixture. Pour into a buttered soufflé dish and cook in a hottish oven, Gas mark 5, 375°F (190°C) for about 25 minutes. Serve instantly.

The Hon. Mrs Sergison-Brooke

GINGER IT UP

Try mixing equal quantities of natural yoghurt and whipped cream and adding freshly grated apple and peeled root ginger with caster sugar to taste. Piled in a bowl and chilled in the fridge, you have a delicious, quickly made dessert.

In fact, a teaspoonful or two of grated fresh ginger adds interest to everything from mincemeat to meringues.

Lady Morse

BROWN AND WHITE STRIPES

A glass bowl filled with this mixture is irresistible. Lightly whip 1½ pt (900 ml) single cream and the same amount of double cream with a teaspoonful of vanilla essence. Mix together 4 oz (100g) bread-crumbs – you can choose whether to use brown or white – 4 oz (l00 g) demerara sugar, 1 tablespoon instant coffee powder and 2 tablespoons of cocoa. Layer in a glass bowl and decorate with grated chocolate. It looks – and tastes – terrific.

Mrs Norman Hudson

THICKER QUICKER

Add a few drops of lemon juice to cream if it refuses to thicken when you are whipping it.

Veronica Hubbard
Housekeeper

CURDLE CURE

If you overbeat cream and it starts to curdle, you might save it if you stop beating and carefully fold full-cream milk (2 tablespoons to 5 fl oz (150 ml) double cream) into the mixture – it helps to stop the separating. Don't use skimmed milk, as it is too thin.

Nikki Kowan-Kedge
Restaurateur, The Loaves and Fishes Restaurant,
Marlborough

YOGHURT

Mix a little cornflour with cold water and add it to yoghurt to stop it curdling in a hot recipe.

Ruth Watson
Chef and Proprietor, The Fox and Goose, Fressingfield

RICHER

Make a richer, smoother, more custardy bread-and-butter pudding by using just egg yolks rather than whole eggs. And always soak the bread in the egg-and-cream mixture for at least half an hour before cooking.

Gary Rhodes
Head Chef, The Greenhouse, London

SOFTER SCOOP

Lemon sorbet is delicious and refreshing but I like this grown-up version for a change, especially in the winter. Make the sorbet in the usual way but add a tablespoonful of whisky to the juice of each lemon. It has the advantage of not only adding flavour but also keeping the sorbet from freezing too hard.

Keryl Hand
Laundress, Katharine House Hospice

SOFTY, SOFTY

To be sure that your homemade ice-cream will be 'soft scoop', add a liqueur such as Drambuie or Tia Maria to the mixture. Alcohol doesn't freeze, so the ice-cream will remain super-soft. NB: only for adult consumption!

Marc Preston
Head Chef, La Fleur de Lys Restaurant, Shaftesbury

OVER-ICED

When the agonizing pain induced by eating too much ice-cream becomes unbearable, you must press a spoon, smooth side down, on to your pulse. The pain goes away immediately. This was taught to me by a Virginian Southern belle who was taught it by her mother in the 1940s.

Lucinda Lambton
Writer and television presenter

A BOWL OF ICE

A gourmet friend once made an ice bowl in which I served dessert. She froze water between two bowls, one inside the other, adding and arranging fresh flowers in a pattern, then adding another layer and repeating the process again. Unmoulding, she put it in warm water until slightly thawed so that the two bowls came away easily, then placed it in the freezer until the time to use it. This contribution to the meal caused such a chorus of admiration that I've never seen any of the guests since.

Maureen Lipman
Author and actress

ABSOLUTELY TOPPING

Crystallized orange zest is the perfect topping for an orange ice or mousse. Scrape the peel of two oranges with a zester over a plate covered with caster sugar so that the oil from the skin lands on the sugar as well as the shreds of peel. Mix together and leave for twenty-four hours. It will become crunchy and absolutely delicious.

The Hon. Mrs Tyser

CHOCOLATE CUPS

Little chocolate cases in which ice-cream or chocolate mousse can be served are not difficult to make. Lightly grease some little paper cake cases. Melt 8 oz (225 g) chocolate in a bowl placed over a pan of simmering water and fill the cups, one at a time, with the chocolate. Place in the fridge for two or three minutes, or until the shell of the chocolate begins to harden at the sides. Pour the remainder of the chocolate back into the bowl and repeat the procedure until it is finished. When the chocolate is quite set, peel the paper away carefully and you will be left with neat little chocolate pots.

G. B. Woodin
Mustard Catering Company

MELTING MOMENTS

The easiest way to melt chocolate is to break it up, put it in a bowl and pour boiling water on it. After about half a minute, pour off the water. You will find the chocolate quite soft and ready to add immediately to the other ingredients – it doesn't dissolve into the water.

The Countess Cathcart

RICHEST

For the easiest, richest, most chocolatey, stickiest chocolate sauce: heat 3 tablespoons of golden syrup and add 4 dessertspoons of Cadbury's Bournville Cocoa. Adjust for taste and for toffeeness and pour directly on to ice-cream.

Dominic Cadbury
Executive Chairman, Cadbury Schweppes

TRANSFORMATION

Transform any brandy butter left over after

Christmas into a really good sauce to go with waffles or pancakes. To every 8 oz (225 g) brandy butter add 2 oz (50 g) roughly chopped pecans or walnuts, 1 fl oz (30 ml) maple syrup and a level teaspoon of ground cinnamon and mix well.

Lorna Wing
Caterer

GOT A LIGHT?

Almost nothing is more depressing than, when the dramatic moment comes for flambéing the Christmas pudding, the brandy won't light. If you pour the spirit into a large metal spoon and heat the underside over a lighter or a match until the spirit has warmed through, when you pour it on to the pudding it will light without fail.

Mrs Lindsay Raywood

THE RIGHT AMOUNT

The quantity of rum called for in a rum sauce recipe is usually the amount found in a miniature bottle. It is worth keeping some of these on the shelf rather than a large bottle.

Neil Gadsby
Honorary Administrator, Katharine House Hospice

IT WON'T FEEL A THING

Ask a favourite nurse (preferably not the one you asked before when you wanted to marinate meat quickly or she may be suspicious of your intentions) for a syringe. Then you can inject black rum into mince pies before heating them up and serving – different amounts for different people, from none for children to nearly a tot for sailors.

Alan Root

NOT SO HARD

Don't throw away left-over caramel that has hardened. It can be reheated without over-cooking by putting it in the microwave – provided it isn't in a metal pan, of course.

Keith Marshall
Chef and Proprietor, The Dew Pond, Old Burghclere

COMING TO THE CRUNCH

For an extra crunchy finish to fruit crumble, sprinkle a layer of soft brown sugar over the topping and bake as usual.

Winifred Cowley
Blackpool landlady

… As a change from an ordinary fruit crumble, try a flapjack mixture on top – delicious!

The Hon. Lady Butler

… For a healthier high-fibre crumble topping, replace half the flour with rolled oats plus a little dried fruit. The sugar should no longer be required.

Dr Eileen Barratt
Nutritionist, Inglewood Health Hydro, Kintbury

PULL OUT A PLUM

Cover, with a scant amount of water, some plums in an earthenware dish. Leave in the simmering oven of the Aga overnight, or for 2–3 hours on the lowest setting of your oven and serve, hot or cold, with cream or ice-cream. The flavour is outstanding.

The Countess Bathurst

STORE CUPBOARD PUDDING

Put some stoned prunes in a jar up to just above half-way mark. Pour in enough sweet white wine to about an inch (2.5 cm) above the fruit. Add a little lemon peel, a clove or two and a bit of cinnamon – and anything else you fancy. Leave for a day or two until the fruit has swollen and absorbed much of the wine. This will keep for ages and is excellent with cream, yoghurt or ice-cream. After about a week you may need to top up the wine level so that the fruit is still covered. The cheapest sweet wine will do for this.

Elisabeth Ray
Journalist

IN THE CAN

All you need for this simple and attractive dessert is a large can of pineapple rings, a jelly (flavour of your choice) and a few glacé cherries. Empty the juice from the can and make up the jelly with it. Pour the mixture back over the pineapple in the tin and leave to set. To serve, pop the can into hot water for a few seconds and slide the contents out longways on to a dish. Decorate with cherries and slice.

Mrs M. Dawson

PEPPERED PINEAPPLE

This way of serving pineapple as a dessert sounds quite alarming but is in fact delicious. Cut a fresh pineapple into slices, removing the outside and taking out the hard middle with your smallest pastry cutter. Then liberally sprinkle freshly ground pepper on to each side of every slice. Arrange attractively on a dish, chill in the fridge for an hour or so and serve with whipped cream.

The Lord Wardington

95

PINEAPPLE TRICKS

Pineapple can be usefully employed in marinades because it contains a pepsin called papain which breaks down protein and so tenderizes meat. It is also said to aid digestion after a rich meal. It should not be used with gelatine because it prevents the gelatine setting although tinned pineapple 'gels' perfectly well.

Lord Tombs of Brailes

PEACHY

For a refreshing dessert, dissolve 6 tablespoons of sugar in 10 fl oz (300 ml) of sweet white wine, skin and slice 6 ripe peaches and submerge them in the liquid. Put in the fridge to get really cold and serve with cream. NB: to skin the peaches, pour boiling water over them and count to ten. Plunge them immediately into cold water and the skins will come away easily.

Mrs Nicholas Hicks

MARSHMALLOW TOPS

Fill canned peach halves with chopped canned pineapple, top with snipped marshmallows and place under a hot grill until the marshmallows turn brown. Serve hot.

Mrs D. M. Skilleten

GOATEE

Put a little pool of honey on to fresh goat's cheese and then, just before serving, pour around a thin syrup made from fructose (fruit sugar) and water boiled until it is caramelized.

The Marchioness of Salisbury

HALF-TIME JELLY

Jelly can be made very quickly if you melt it in a microwave with half the required liquid and then top up with ice-cubes.

Mr G. FitzGerald

JUICY JELLY

Six or eight large warmed oranges will make 1 pt (600 ml) of fresh juice. Add a sachet of gelatine according to the instructions on the packet and make a delicious and simple jelly.

The Lady Hylton

GRAPE IDEA

To cut grapes in half quickly for a fruit salad etc., hold ten or fifteen under the palm of your hand on a chopping board and carefully cut across the fruit under your hand with a long carving knife.

Marc Preston
Head Chef, La Fleur de Lys Restaurant, Shaftesbury

JUICY

Hard oranges and lemons yield little juice, but if you cut them in half and microwave on the highest setting for 15 seconds they will juice much better.

Sheila Black
Journalist

SHINY

To make a fruit coulis (a fresh-fruit sauce) which is glazed, boil it for just a few seconds with some icing sugar and a little lemon juice. Preparing the coulis the day before makes it taste even more delicious.

Lady Palumbo

BEFORE THE SQUEEZE

To extract the maximum amount of juice from an orange or lemon, before squeezing, roll it on a table top beneath a firm hand.

Derek Collins

PEELING

To remove the peel and pith from an orange, immerse it in boiling water for up to four minutes. Then, using a knife or your thumb, you will find that the peel and pith come away very easily.

Dame Betty Boothroyd
The Speaker, House of Commons

A TOUCH OF FROST

Frosted green grapes look festive and taste delicious. All you do is dip the grapes (seedless, of course) one by one in beaten egg white, shake off the surplus, then – and this is the secret – *roll* them in caster sugar until evenly coated. Lay them out on silicone paper to dry thoroughly before serving.

Laurie Purden
Journalist

… Frosted redcurrants decorate a dish. Dip the fruit on their stalks into lightly whipped egg white and then shake them about in a plastic bag with caster sugar. Lay them carefully on kitchen paper to dry.

Vikki Sikking
Voluntary fundraiser, Katharine House Hospice

FRUIT SALAD

When making a fruit salad, chop, cut or slice all

the fruit that is likely to go brown – such as bananas, apples and pears – into lemon juice, turning the pieces as you put them in. Then add the other fruit and syrup.

Eleanor Hudson

TAKE THE PIP

My wife says that when making apple purée, in order to improve the flavour and to avoid disappointment, you should put the whole apple in, including the pips, and sieve when it is cooked.

Lord Oaksey
Racing correspondent and commentator

CUT AND DRIED

Core and peel some apples and slice them thickly. Lay them out on a cake rack and dry them in the simmering oven of the Aga, or a cool oven, Gas mark ¼, 225°F (110°C) for several hours. They make delicious nibbles, either plain or added to nuts and raisins and served with drinks.

The Countess Bathurst

STRAWBERRY TIME

Never hull strawberries before you wash them. Rinse them under a cold tap in a colander. Gently roll them about on kitchen paper to dry. Save them, covered, on a flat plate in the fridge until they are needed and hull them just before serving.

To improve the flavour, slice, marinate in and serve with fresh orange juice.

Mary Whiting
Food writer and teacher

EASY FREEZE

Each summer I buy twelve plastic punnets of Scottish raspberries from Marks & Spencer when they are at their best. Without opening the punnets, I wrap each one separately in plenty of aluminium foil to keep them air-tight and put them straight in the deep freeze. They come out six months later exactly like fresh raspberries. So easy!

Betty Kenward
Formerly of 'Jennifer's Diary', Harpers and Queen

STRAWBERRY PICKLE

Pickling strawberries makes a nice change from turning them into jam and they are an attractive accompaniment to lots of cold dishes. Boil 5 lb (2.2 kg) sugar with 1 pt (750 ml) vinegar and when it is boiling throw in 6 lb (2.6 kg) strawberries, which must be firm and fresh. Simmer for about 20 minutes and pot up into sterilized, hot glass jars.

Mrs Mildred Nash

PASSIONATE

When buying passion fruit look for the ones that are 'on the shrivel'. If they are too smooth the fruit won't be ripe enough and if too wrinkly they will be over-ripe and could be dry.

Angela Rawson
Restaurateur, The Loaves and Fishes Restaurant, Marlborough

TEASMADE

Soak dried fruit such as prunes and apricots in tea. I use Earl Grey or jasmine, hot, just covering the fruit. When they are softened, cook them in the tea with brown sugar and blanched almonds. Serve for breakfast or later in the day with thick cream.

Caroline Conran
Food writer

SCOOPY

In order to prepare medlars for jam, pick them at the end of October and allow to blet (soften). Then, to extract the flesh, grip the flat end (*cul de cheval!*), make a fine incision across the pointed end and scoop the flesh away with the back of the knife, thus leaving skin and five hard stones behind.

Caroline Holmes
Lecturer and demonstrator, Gourmet Gardening

BEGINNER'S LUCK

If you have never made marmalade before, beware – it's a sticky business! First clear the kitchen ready for action. Then assemble equipment – Magimix, plates, knives, wooden spoons, etc. Then cover the floor with newspaper, several layers so that as they get messy or ruffled you only have to remove the top one.

You also need rubber gloves, plastic apron, two J-cloths and two very old J-cloths or rags, a roll of kitchen paper, about a dozen 10 in (25 cm) squares of old linen and some bits of string so that you can tie up the pips. And a sink full of hot water – for constant washing.

And TIME and PATIENCE. Good luck!

Mrs Geoffrey Holbech

LIQUEUR MARMALADE

When my marmalade is made, just before it's potted up, I add a slug of Cointreau or Grand Marnier – or sometimes just whatever liqueur comes to hand – to give it an extra-special flavour.

Lord Montagu of Beaulieu

SKIN ALONE

We squeeze lots of oranges for fresh orange juice. We save the skins in the freezer and make marmalade at a later date following a traditional Seville orange marmalade recipe but adding a couple of grapefruit to compensate for the lack of acidity in the sweet oranges.

Christopher and Joanna Wickens
Chefs and Proprietors, Wickens, Northleach

THROW A DISC

It can be fun to make your own wax discs to cover homemade jam. Simply melt white candle sticks (old stubs will do), and pour the resulting wax on to the top of the hot jam. When the wax is cool there will be nice removable discs. Cover with lids in the usual way.

Mrs Francis Sitwell

FIRELIGHTERS FOR NOTHING

Any citrus peel will dry in the Aga's coolest oven (or on a baking sheet in the airing cupboard or on a radiator) and will make very good firelighters. Ecology-conscious children may enjoy coating the dried peel with melted candle wax.

The Lady Hylton

CAKES, BREAD AND PASTRY

Some gave them white bread and some gave them brown,
And some gave them plum cake and sent them out of town.

LEWIS CARROLL

NOOKS AND CRANNIES

Before baking a cake, instead of buttering the tin you can save time by using a pastry brush and a light tasteless oil – groundnut is very good – to get quickly into the corners and cracks.

Ruth Watson
Chef and Proprietor, The Fox and Goose Inn, Fressingfield

… Another way to prepare a cake tin quickly: butter the inside of the tin thoroughly, press the lining paper into place until well coated, then lift out and replace butter side up.

Geraldene Holt
Food writer

TIME SAVER

Forget the traditional way of making a cake – first creaming the butter and sugar etc. Try melting the butter or margarine in a saucepan (not too hot) and meanwhile dump the eggs and sugar together in a bowl and beat with an electric whisk until really thick and mousse-like. Then pour in the melted butter, beating as you go. Finally add the flour, with the beater on at slow – you need a light touch at this point. This will produce a perfect, well-risen cake and takes half the time and a quarter of the effort.

Lady Gage

LIGHTER

Add a generous teaspoon of jelly marmalade to a Victoria sponge mixture, making sure it is well incorporated into the other ingredients. Not only does this give the cake a delicious flavour, but it also helps to keep it moist. And instead of adding milk to make a dropping consistency, add boiling water. This will make the cake much lighter.

Katie Boyle
TV personality

SUBSTITUTION

For an extra light cake, take one tablespoonful of flour out of the mixture – well, don't put it in –

and substitute a tablespoonful of cornflour.

Mrs Harold Osher

MOST MOIST

When baking rich fruitcakes, which need a prolonged period in the oven, moisten one hand with cold water. Press the damp, but not wet, knuckles all over the top of the cake mixture in the tin before baking. This keeps the top of the cake beautifully moist.

Marguerite Patten
Cookery writer

PLUMP AND BEAUTIFUL

It can be very annoying to find that the recipe for the cake you want to make immediately calls for the dried fruit to be soaked overnight. But if you pop them in the microwave in whatever juice is needed for a couple of minutes, they will plump up beautifully.

Mrs F. Nelson

THAT SINKING FEELING

Avoid the raisins etc. sinking to the bottom of a rich fruitcake by rolling the fruit in sugar or some flour before adding it to the cake.

Roland Klein
Designer

KING ALFRED SHOULD HAVE KNOWN

Should you burn your cakes all you have to do to make them presentable is to scrub off the burnt part with a nutmeg grater.

Mrs Mary Tolley

TRICKY TREAT

I'm always *forced* by my children to 'make' a Christmas cake. Making a cake takes a *day*; marzipan an afternoon and royal icing another; plus you have to remember to give yourself a day in hand *three months* before Christmas. My birthday is 25 September and I swim in guilt every Sunday afterwards, right through Advent. So now I buy a 3 lb (1.5 kg) heavy fruitcake either from Fortnum & Mason or Marks & Spencer, depending on funds (the children can't tell the difference, though I can) and strip off the icing and almond paste – often not until Christmas Eve. Then I laboriously make real marzipan and real icing and plaster it on in a suitably *au naturel* and homemade fashion. No one is allowed to cut it until Boxing Day. It's just long enough if you harden it off in the warming oven of the Aga. 'Gosh,' says *tout le monde*, 'how do you find the *time?*'

Vicki Woods
Editor, Harpers and Queen

PAPER PATTERNS

For a quick decoration on top of a cake, cover the top with a doily and sprinkle it with icing sugar. Take the doily off very carefully and you are left with a lovely pattern.

The Marchioness of Zetland

SWEET LITTLE SPRINKLER

The advent of the tea-bag has rendered the tea-strainer redundant. But get it out from the back of the cupboard; it is just the thing for sprinkling icing sugar individually on to little buns and cakes.

Sandra Hendley

SUPER SMOOTH

If you're rolling out sugar paste to the correct size for

covering a cake, don't actually roll it – *pull* the rolling pin across the paste in four directions in order to get a *perfect smooth finish*. However expert you are at rolling there's always a ripple caused by uneven pressure one way or the other.

Andrée Massey
The Icing Parlour, York

IN JUG

To fill a piping bag quickly, put the bag in a jug and fold the top over the edge of the jug.

Mrs Betty Barclay

JUST A LITTLE

Use only natural, edible colours in icing. And don't add too much: transfer the colour from the bottle to the icing on the end of a skewer or cocktail stick, a drop at a time. As with colour, so with flavour – too much will overpower the taste of the cake.

Elisabeth Phillips-Smith
Matron, Katharine House Hospice

CAKE-WRITING

Confectioners' pens which are used for writing on icing often dry out. They can be revived (can't we all?) by a dip in gin or vodka.

Serena Jackson
Cookery writer

CURLY TOPS

Chocolate curls to decorate the top of a cake or mousse are easily made by scraping a chocolate bar with a potato peeler.

Mrs Mary Tolley

DRIZZLE

If you want to drizzle melted chocolate on to the top of a cake or pudding, do it the easy way. Break up a chocolate bar and put it in a polythene bag. Microwave for a few moments and cut a tiny hole in a corner of the bag. It is easy to squeeze the chocolate through the hole and pour it in an even stream.

Peggy Osher

TOFFEE NUTS

Here's a quick and easy decoration for cakes and puddings: caramelized hazelnuts. Boil the nuts for two minutes, drain well and roll in caster sugar until well coated. Cook in a deep-fat fryer for three to four minutes and you will have golden-brown caramelized hazelnuts. You can do this with walnuts and almonds too.

Marc Preston
Chef and Proprietor, La Fleur de Lys Restaurant,
Shaftesbury

KEEP IT MOIST

A fruitcake will keep moist if you put an eating apple into the tin with it when storing.

Mrs B. S. Barlow

SQUIRRELLING

Nuts are better bought in small quantities and used up quickly. Any left over should not be stored in a metal container as the metal causes them to go off more quickly. They are best kept in the refrigerator or freezer.

Sophie Grigson
Food writer

PODS

Vanilla pods stored in an air-tight jar with caster sugar will make vanilla sugar and keep the pods fresh.

Keith Marshall
Chef and Proprietor, The Dew Pond, Old Burghclere

SUGAR CRISP

Biscuits will remain crisp if you put a lump of sugar into the tin with them.

Veronica Hubbard
Housekeeper

TWO FOR ONE

The first slice of cake is always the most difficult to detach and transport to the plate intact. If you cut *two* slices in the beginning, one will come away easily.

Emma Lubbock
Accountant

STEAMING

When baking bread at home you can replicate, to some extent, the effect of a commercial steam-injected oven by putting a pan of boiling water into the oven with the loaf. And spray the bread before and during baking with a water-spray such as you would use to squirt flowers. This gives a lighter crust, especially if the bread is baked at a high temperature.

Colin White
Head Chef, Woolley Grange Hotel, Bradford-on-Avon

SOURED

Every keen baker should know that if you mix natural (untreated) whole milk or low-fat natural yoghurt with water or milk in equal parts you will make soured milk – marvellous for mixing soda bread or scones. But never use heat-treated milk that has turned sour – it's not the same.

Katie Stewart
Cookery writer

PILOT LIGHT

I live in Japan now and can't find any bread that isn't made with glutinous white flour or full of sugar. So I make my own but having no airing cupboard or Aga I was stumped to find a place to rise the dough. Now I've discovered that if I put it in the gas oven in a Pyrex bowl covered with cling film with just the pilot light on (if you have a gas oven) it rises perfectly. Otherwise, put your electric oven on 300°F (150°C) for 10 minutes, then turn it off. There should be enough residual heat to rise the dough perfectly if you put it in now.

Mrs Alexander Pease

CRISPY CRUST

My wife and I like really crusty loaves and, since we now make our own bread, we achieve the perfect finish by putting the loaf back in the turned-off oven after we have taken it out of the tin.

Neil Gadsby
Honorary Administrator, Katharine House Hospice

HANDY

While making pastry, bread or anything that

involves getting flour etc. all over your hands, keep a couple of plastic bags handy to thrust your hands into when the telephone rings – which it inevitably will.

Sheila Black
Journalist

IT'S GOOD TO BE ROUGH

Choose long wooden rolling pins without handles. A slight roughness is good because the grains of flour will stick to it better.

Mary Whiting
Food writer and teacher

BETWEEN THE SHEETS

Roll pastry out between sheets of greaseproof paper – no board or table to be cleaned.

Teresa Smith

NICER

Rice flour is a much more agreeable and effective medium for dusting the pastry board and for handling pastry generally than plain flour or cornflour. It also makes a good easy-to-blend *beurre manié* for thickening sauces.

Maggie Black
Food historian

CRUMBS

I make double the flour and fat mixture when I'm making shortcrust pastry. Then I freeze the excess at crumb stage before adding water. It thaws very quickly and can be used for fruit crumble as well.

Mrs Sheila Page

HIGH RISE

When you have cut the discs out of puff pastry for vol-au-vents, turn each one upside-down. This will help the pastry to rise – because of the action of the cutter edge on the pastry.

Rory Kennedy
Executive Chef, Hanbury Manor, Ware

INSTANT TART

A pastry tart-case straight from the freezer thaws perfectly when filled with hot stewed or sautéed buttery fruit just before serving.

Geraldene Holt
Food writer

FLAT OUT

I used to press down the base of a pastry case with the back of a spoon. Now I have found a better way: I use my potato-masher – a much flatter finish.

Sandra Hendley

TANG

A layer of marmalade added to custard tarts – spread on the pastry before baking – will give them a lovely tangy flavour.

The Marchioness of Zetland

LIFT OFF

It can be quite tricky lifting a blind-baked pastry case which is going to have an uncooked filling away from the flan ring. If, after greasing the flan tin, you sprinkle it with fine breadcrumbs there won't be a problem.

James Graham
Chef and Proprietor, Ostlers Close, Cupar

NO LEAKS

After blind-baking a pastry case for a quiche, brush the base and sides with egg wash and pop it back in the oven for a few seconds. The egg wash will set and prevent leaking.

Rory Kennedy
Executive Chef, Hanbury Manor, Ware

TIPSY CAKE

Gather together a cup of butter, four large eggs, a cup of dried fruit, a teaspoon of baking soda, a teaspoon of salt, a cup of brown sugar, lemon juice, nuts and a bottle of whisky.

First sample the whisky to check for quality. Take a large bowl and check the whisky again: to be sure that it is of the highest quality, pour one level cup and drink. Repeat.

Turn on the electric mixer, beat the butter in a large fluffy bowl. Add one spoontea of sugar and beat again. Make sure the whisky is still OK. Cry another tup.

Turn off mixer. Break two leggs and add to the bowl and chuck in the dried fruit. Mix on the burner. If the fruit gets stuck in the beaters, pry it loose with a drewscriver. Sample the whisky again for tonsisticly.

Next, sift two cups of salt – or something, who cares? Check the whisky. Now sift the lemon juice and strain your nuts. Add one babblespoon of brown sugar, or whatever colour you can find. Mix well. Grease the oven. Turn the cake pan to 30 gredees. Don't forget to beat off the timer. Throw the bowl out of the window, check the whisky again and go to bed.

Lord Aberconway

SUPPERS, SNACKS AND SOUFFLÉS

For my part, I consider supper a turnpike through which I must pass, in order to get to bed.

OLIVER EDWARDS

SAUSAGE SPECIAL

For a really easy-to-make, satisfying supper dish take 1 lb (450 g) of sausage meat, 1 lb (450 g) of Bramley apples, 1 lb (450 g) of onions and some sliced tomatoes. In a deep casserole put alternate layers of sausage meat (rolled out to fit on a floured board), sliced apples and sliced onions, ending with sausage meat. Cover and bake in a moderate oven, Gas mark 5, 375°F (190°C), for 45 minutes, cover with sliced tomatoes and cook for a further 10 minutes uncovered.

Rt. Hon. Gillian Shephard MP

MORE THAN ONE MEAT BALL

To produce juicy and tender meatballs I always add

114

two large slices of bread to each pound of raw meat. This is the easy-peasy way to mix them. Purée the bread with half a medium onion in the food processor or blender, adding a large sprig of parsley, half a teaspoon of salt, 15 grinds of black pepper and a teaspoon of dark soy sauce. Mix with 1 lb (450 g) raw beef and work together with a fork. Leave for 30 minutes, then shape and cook as you wish.

Evelyn Rose
Cookery writer

GROWN-UP

A splash of last night's left-over red wine makes Sunday supper's tinned beans taste much more grown-up.

Rosemary Stark
Food writer

SUMMER SUPPER

One of my favourite 'healthy' summer suppers is a seared chicken salad. Cut two chicken breasts into slices and marinate in some crushed garlic, olive oil, salt and pepper. Cook 6 oz (175 g) of pasta twirls while you are preparing the rest of the salad. Whisk together 2 tablespoons of white wine vinegar with 6 tablespoons of olive oil and season to taste. Wash and halve a punnet of cherry tomatoes and add to the vinaigrette with plenty of basil or chives. Heat a non-stick frying pan until it is very hot and sear the chicken slices on both sides until cooked through. They shouldn't need any extra oil. Add to the tomatoes, tossing in the hot pasta and a few cubes of soft goat's cheese. Serves three.

Sybil Kapoor
Food writer

NICE TO HANDLE

Stuffed pancakes are a versatile supper stand-by. But the batter for them is better made with strong (bread) flour, which will make the pancakes easier to handle.

Elisabeth Collett
Food studies lecturer

EGGS AND ONIONS

Eggs and onions go well together and this simple version of Oeufs à la Tripe is no exception. Hard-boil some eggs and fry the same weight of onions, sliced, in butter until they are translucent. Sprinkle the onions with flour, mix in well and add milk to make a fairly thick onion sauce. Peel and slice the eggs and layer them with the onion mixture in an ovenproof dish. Top with grated cheese and brown briefly in a medium oven.

Jo Cornley
Bursar, Katharine House Hospice

HOT STUFF

Any left-over potatoes should be mashed in a frying pan with a dollop of good curry paste and plenty of fried onion. When cold they make a superb savoury spread for toast, either as a snack, starter or on a picnic.

Christopher Gable
Artistic Director, Northern Ballet Theatre

PIN PRICKS

It makes a nice change to boil an egg this way. Prick both ends with a pin (a good early-morning start for a steady hand). Place it in cold water, bring it to the boil and leave to boil for a further minute. With luck, no cracks in the shell and a perfect result inside.

Ted Dexter
Test cricketer

STOPPING THE LEAK

It is maddening when you find that the egg you are about to boil has a crack in it – especially if it is an expensive gull's egg. Painting the crack with lemon juice solves the problem – no leaking of the white when boiling.

Carmen Lleô
Professional cook

POACHING QUAIL'S EGGS

Put 5 fl oz (15 ml) of white wine vinegar in a bowl. Using a small, sharp knife, slice the fat top off the quail's eggs and pour into the vinegar. When you have sufficient eggs leave them for fifteen minutes. Bring a pan of water to the boil, pour in the eggs with the vinegar and reboil. Depending on how firm you like your eggs, remove sooner or later. Cool the eggs in iced water.

Sonia Kidney
Chef and Proprietor, The Marsh Goose Restaurant,
Moreton-in-Marsh

HOLD THE WHITE

Sometimes when you are poaching an egg the white swirls away all over the place. If you use absolutely fresh eggs this won't happen, but you can make doubly sure by adding a little malt vinegar to the water.

Ann Morrison

EGGSTRA

I can recommend macaroni cheese with the addition of chopped hard-boiled eggs and tinned tomatoes.

Andrea Newman
Writer

AN EXTRA EGG

For perfect scrambled eggs, always add one extra egg to the quantity required. When the eggs are nearly cooked, beat in the extra egg, raw, and stir for a few moments. This gives a really rich egg flavour.

Sir Hardy Amies
Designer

CREAMIER

I have a way of making scrambled eggs creamier: instead of adding milk or cream, after beating them I put them in a saucepan with melted butter until almost cooked. I then add the juice of half a lemon, cook for three seconds, remove from the heat and the eggs will have taken on a creamy consistency.

Pamela, Lady Harlech

DISTINGUISHED

Scrambled eggs are usually a bit sickly and my way of making them much more appetizing is as follows: spread Marmite on buttered toast or, even better, on a buttered crumpet and pile the egg mixture on top. The effect is to transform an everyday dish into a savoury of distinction.

Sir Peregrine Worsthorne

RICH ECONOMY

Having invested a king's ransom in a truffle, make the most of it. Put it in an air-tight box with half a dozen eggs for 24 hours and the eggs will absorb the truffle flavour. Then that great delicacy, scrambled eggs with truffles, can be made with a fraction of extravagance, using very little truffle.

Mrs Bryan Jenks

DON'T LOOK BACK

When Mrs Beeton's recipes call for a dozen eggs, remember that in her day eggs were much, much smaller and that almost certainly six large ones would be the equivalent today.

Lisa Smith
Assistant Cook, Katharine House Hospice

EGGS OCTAVIAN

I think I have invented this way of making a fried egg a special treat. Splash Worcestershire sauce into the butter – it *must* be butter – while they are cooking. Sensational!

Octavian von Hofmannsthal
Art publisher

FOREVER SOFT

An egg which has been soft-boiled or poached and allowed to cool cannot be cooked again to become hard. Thus it can be safely reheated for various recipes, for instance, Eggs in an Overcoat. Make an omelette, peel soft-boiled eggs and reheat, place the eggs on the unfolded omelette and place another one, also unfolded, over them. NB: the soft-boiled eggs should be used the same day.

HKH Princess Lilian of Sweden

BEST SOLDIERS

The best soldiers with which to eat boiled eggs are made with toasted pitta bread – they don't go floppy.

Mary Franklin
aged three

SIMPLE SEPARATION

In order to separate the white of an egg from the yolk easily, break the egg into a saucer and start to tip the egg into a bowl. As it slithers across the surface, catch the yolk in an egg cup. It is a totally brilliant method which never breaks the yolk and which succeeds every time.

Esther Rantzen
Television presenter

QUICK WHISK

If possible, use a copper bowl for whisking egg whites. They whisk more quickly and become firmer.

Peter Kromberg
Executive Chef, Hotel Inter-Continental, London

A LITTLE SUPPORT

When whisking egg whites for a savoury soufflé, which don't have any sugar added to support them, add a teaspoon of lemon juice once the whites have reached soft peak stage. This will prevent them from becoming grainy and separating.

Allan Holland
Chef and Proprietor, Mallory Court, Leamington Spa

SOFTER

When making a soufflé, don't beat the egg whites

until they are really firm. A softer texture will rise quicker and higher.

Julia Hughes
Catering Manager, Forest Mere, Liphook

GET A RISE

If you want to ensure that a soufflé will rise, add an extra egg white.

Lady Cowdray

SOUFFLÉ WISDOM

To ensure the lightness of a soufflé and to prevent it from collapsing as it leaves the oven, substitute 1 oz (25 g) of cornflour for 1 oz (25 g) of flour.

With sweet soufflés, such as a soufflé Grand Marnier, rather than incorporate the liqueur with the mixture, soak three small sponge fingers with the liqueur and insert into the middle of the soufflé dish before topping up with the mixture.

Always use the basic soufflé mixture, whether savoury or sweet, when it is still hot. The soufflés will rise higher and have a better texture.

Peter Kromberg
Executive Chef, Hotel Inter-Continental, London

COLD ROUX

For success with soufflés and to be sure that they don't sink on arrival at the table, make sure that the roux is absolutely cold before adding the egg yolks. The eggs should not start to cook until they hit the heat of the oven. Believe me, this way the soufflé will remain firm and not flop.

Gerry Harvey
Chef and Proprietor, Middle Piccadilly, Sherborne

READY AND WAITING

If you are a cook-hostess and you want to serve a soufflé at the end of a meal, be it cheese or chocolate, prepare it in the morning (yes, egg whites as well) and put it in the fridge – don't cook it. It will wait peacefully until you are about to serve the course before the soufflé. At that moment pop it in a hot oven and it will be ready, beautifully risen, when you want it. I find this works best with a four-person mixture, so if I am entertaining eight guests I make two soufflés.

Mrs John Boughey

POTTED CHEESE

Here is a useful way of using up remains of cheeses. Hard cheese, soft cheese, French or English – all may be used in a careful combination. Try to combine a sharp cheese with a mild one, or a hard cheese with a creamy one. Simply combine pieces of cheese with butter and/or cream, and sherry, vermouth or white wine in the food processor, in the following proportions: 3 parts cheese, 1 part butter (or half butter and half double cream) and one part alcohol. Process until blended, then stir in 1 part chopped chives and pile into small jars. Chill and serve with crusty French bread or toast.

Arabella Boxer
Food writer

GRATED CHEESE

You can keep grated cheese for several days if you wrap it in a cloth which has been soaked in salted water.

Roland Klein
Designer

INSTANT RIPENING

To ripen a hard Camembert or Brie cheese, set the microwave oven to defrost and switch on for 30 seconds – this is for a 3 oz (75 g) piece.

Mrs B. S. Barlow

HERBAL

Make scones in the usual way but add lots of herbs – chopped chives, parsley, etc., to the mixture. Serve them hot with cheese instead of biscuits.

Beth Williams

ANY OLD RIND

This is a good way to use up odd pieces of cheese and cheese crust. Grate or process ½ lb (225 g) and add ½ pint (300 ml) milk. Stir and put in the oven until the milk forms a curd. Take it out and mix in a well-beaten egg. Return it to the oven until it sets. Delicious on toast or with bacon.

Milly Yates
Professional cook

DEVILLED BISCUITS

My father always insisted on a savoury and I was delighted to find one of his, and my, favourites in his old cook's recipe book. It was delicious and looks very simple to make. Smear butter on to Carr's water biscuits, with a little curry powder, a small dollop of chutney and top with grated cheese. Leave in a hot oven or under the grill for about 10 minutes.

James Price QC

PARTIES, PICNICS AND BARBECUES

*The best number for a dinner party is two – myself
and a dam' good head waiter.*

Nubar Gulbenkian

HOME SWEET HOME

A dinner party shouldn't try to reflect a restaurant
meal. One is a commercial enterprise in which
choice of dishes and eating time has to be offered
in order to justify the appearance of a nasty bill at
the end of the proceedings. At home you have the
good sense to decide these things in advance.

Shaun Hill
Head Chef, Gidleigh Park, Chagford

SAY CHEESE

For a truly encouraging smell emanating from the kitchen as a welcome to guests, try sprinkling Parmesan cheese on anything you can think of, including the slow hotplate of the Aga. It beats roasting coffee and freshly baked bread any day, and the supermarkets haven't discovered it yet, either.

Simone Sekers
Food writer

TAKE IT EASY

At many tables, especially in the country, a dinner is presented which obviously reflects huge labours by the hostess, whose ambitions have outreached her abilities. If she focused more energy on securing first-rate ingredients and spent less time in the kitchen, she would come to the table less exhausted and her guests would go home happier.

Max Hastings
Editor-in-Chief, Daily Telegraph

HIDE YOUR LIGHT

When having people round to dinner, don't make the mistake of doing things too well or you'll never be asked back to their place. If you're not a gourmet cook, don't pretend to be one. Make a few deliberate mistakes, apologize a lot and be far too red-faced and agitated to enjoy any conversation on food. This way most of the women present will take pity on your husband and you'll be invited out a lot.

Maureen Lipman
Actress and author

STARVE 'EM

To ensure the success of any meal, serve it so late that your guests are ravenous. Even the simplest food – bangers and mash, spaghetti and butter, cabbage and rice pudding (not altogether) – will taste good to those who have given up all hope of ever eating again.

Rachel Billington
Author

PING!

In the absence of someone in the kitchen I always wear a pre-set egg-timer hidden on a string round my neck. This enables me to relax in conversation, and when it goes off has the instant effect of getting guests into the dining-room quickly. Very useful when serving soufflés as a first course.

Angela Darling
Interior designer

LONELY

When I need help clearing the table at large informal meals I enlist it by announcing, at the end of each course, a different category of person to help: i.e. 'anyone still at school', 'all ladies under fifty', 'anyone with grey hair', etc. This summer I announced 'anyone who has been divorced', and found myself left alone at the table except for one fourteen-year-old boy.

Lady Edmonstone

SITTING COMFORTABLY

If your dinner guests (like mine) are talkative, dawdle in the dining-room and take a long time eating the first course while they discuss the decadence of the nation, it is useless to have a main course which needs perfect timing. A fillet of beef will be ruined. I suggest putting your main culinary effort into the first course and serving something very simple (even a cold dish) afterwards. If you think this is too austere, you can have a hot dessert – flambéed bananas won't come to much harm in the oven even if your guests get on to the health service.

Remember, every dinner that is not a frightful failure takes twice as long to be eaten as you expect.

Anne Scott-James
Journalist

DINNER-PARTY DISASTER

If your soufflé has collapsed or your oven broken down and your guests are already seated and hungry, simply run outside the house and chuck a brick through the sitting-room window, preferably wrapped in some offensive remarks. While your guests are sweeping the floor and calling the police you can cut a large pile of sandwiches and dish up the cocoa.

Victoria Wood
Comedienne

DON'T PANIC

When you drop, as I did, your starter course on the floor when all your dinner guests are seated waiting for your delicious food, you just have to take a deep breath, put a large smile on your face and sweep into the dining-room saying there will be a short interval, pour more wine, chat madly and keep smiling.

Lady Connell

ASK YOUR BEST FRIEND

Always invite a best friend if you are giving a largish dinner party, and ask her (or him) to bring either the starter or the pudding. They won't mind a bit and will make a huge effort. This enables you to put all your skill and energy into the rest. You get the best of two worlds and half the hassle! Be sure to discuss the menu with them, though, to get the balance right.

Gina Fratini
Designer

FAVOURING FATTIES

Fat people make better guests and you are wise to consider inviting persons who are a touch greedy and over-indulgent. People who don't enjoy food make poor reward for all your effort and those who are laden with allergies or neuroses over what they can or cannot eat are better off anyway directed to the nearest clinic!

Shaun Hill
Head Chef, Gidleigh Park, Chagford

TESTING, TESTING

Never test new dishes on your guests; they are not there as guinea-pigs. Let your family or long-trusted friends help you with some honest criticism first. Your social life will not suffer (family and friends soon forget but a disastrous dinner party lingers long in the memories of disappointed guests). More importantly, you will be familiar with the recipe and find you can prepare it better and faster, knowing the pitfalls and difficulties.

Raymond Blanc
*Chef and Proprietor, Le Manoir aux Quat'Saisons,
Great Milton*

NEAT

If you're making sandwiches for lots of people, use a food processor to mince the fillings together with the butter. Grated cheese and beetroot is popular with children (because of the colour), or mustard and ham, or salmon and cream cheese. Spread these straight on to sliced bread, cut off the crusts and repack back into the plastic bread bag. Freeze until required. They store well in the freezer, being square and neatly packed.

Janet
Alice Thomas Ellis's nanny

THROW-AWAY SHOES

If you have to give a once-in-a-lifetime party when the guests have to park in a field and where mud and cowpats present a problem, get the man at the gate to hand out throw-away overshoes. They are easily obtainable since they are used in food factories and industrial workshops. They can then be discarded at the front door.

Gervase Jackson-Stops

SMOKEY

In the summer, if we have lots of people to entertain in connection with events such as the music festival, we often cook on a large barbecue. Rather than use bought hickory chips to create that special flavour, we use our own prunings that have been saved throughout the year. Apple wood or quince works well for pork kebabs, rosemary cuttings for chicken, philadelphus for fish etc. As well as the distinctive flavouring, a wonderful aroma wafts through the air, reminiscent of outdoor feasting in ages past.

The Lady Ashcombe

CHECK OUT

Check list for the perfect picnic:

Corkscrew
Bottle/can opener
Sharp knife
Napkins/paper
   towels/wet wipes
Bag for rubbish

Insect repellent/sting
   cream/sun cream
Something to sit on
Games for children
   (ball or frisbee)
Windbreak, sunshade
   (or umbrella!)

Add your own necessities – only you know which one-eyed teddy or intergalactic spaceship is crucial to the peace of the afternoon.

Jane Asher
Actress

PREPARING FOR THE BARBECUE

Use lots of coal – don't be mean, even though it's expensive – and when lighting it fifty minutes before you start cooking always remember to use three or four firelighters as well as the normal ignition fuel. You will have no failures and no recriminations from starving guests.

Richard Briers
Actor

DOWSER

It's always useful to have a plastic container, such as an old Fairy Liquid bottle, filled with water to damp down the flames caused by dripping fat. And if the barbecue is large enough, keeping part of the charcoal cooler than the rest provides a good place to put food that is cooking too fast, or that just needs to be kept warm.

Alistair Neilson

SAFE SAUSAGES

Ever struggled with sausages spinning on a skewer? Simply fix them with two skewers, slotting on several. This way they are easy to turn and you can just push them off on to hot plates.

Katie Stewart
Food writer

BARBECUE CLUE

Start cooking only when the charcoal has turned to a soft, white-hot ash. If feeling adventurous, pour four drops of virgin olive oil on to the charcoal so that its fumes augment the flavour of the fillet steaks. When your guests are becoming restive, serve the wonderful-smelling, smoking meat, open up the red wine and pour lavishly, talking wittily and, probably, shrilly, the while. *Do not on any account* eat any of the barbecued meat yourself: it will be partly burnt and partly dangerously raw. Have something eggy in the kitchen when they've all gone home.

Frank Muir
Writer and broadcaster

OUTDOOR STEW

A novel way to have a nice hot meal outside. Line a large wooden box with straw and place a one-pot meal such as an Irish stew in a casserole with the lid on. Cover with lots more straw and the stew will carry on cooking and be nice and hot when required.

Alan Craigie
Chef and Proprietor, Creel Restaurant, Orkney

WINES, SPIRITS AND
SOFT DRINKS

There are three reasons why we drink:
Good wine – a friend – or being dry –
Or lest we should be by and by –
Or any other reason why.

HENRY ALDRICH

NOT WITH A BANG

To stop a bottle of champagne exploding – as it often does after a bumpy journey – tap the bottom firmly.

The Dowager Marchioness of Reading

POP

This patent method of opening a champagne bottle was taught to me by James Smith, the genial General Manager of the Hong Kong Hilton. First, take one sabre. Then, holding the bottle on the palm of one's left hand, run the sabre with a smooth action from the base of the bottle up to the rim that goes round the neck. If enough energy is applied the cork, the foil, the wire *et al* will come off cleanly! It takes but a trice and tastes frightfully nice.

Derek Nimmo
Actor

SPARKLE

If you don't finish a bottle of champagne, put it in the fridge (even without a cork) and after two or three days it will still sparkle when poured.

Sir Hardy Amies
Designer

COCKTAIL TIME

The essential ingredient for a summer party is a champagne cocktail. It must be pressed into the hand of each arriving guest and without fail people will feel deliciously spoilt and lose their initial shyness. Place a sugar cube in the base of a champagne flute. Sprinkle with two drops of Angostura bitters and then just cover with a good brandy. Fill the rest with your favourite dry champagne.

Sybil Kapoor
Food writer

FROZEN FRUIT

A cup based on champagne, white wine or cider will look even more inviting if it is served in a glass which has an ice-cube with a cherry (or other soft fruit) encased within it.

Arabella Boxer
Food writer

133

INSTANT CHAMBRÉ

To 'chambré' claret in an emergency before decanting it, remove the foil cover from the cork and lay the bottle in the microwave on a damp cloth – this is to steady it. Switch on to defrost for two and a half minutes.

J. E. H. Collins

TAKING THE TEMPERATURE

Remember that unless you have a proper wine cellar, red wines may need cooling down slightly before serving. 'Room temperature' doesn't mean the temperature of today's typical centrally heated rooms: it usually means 16–18°C. A bottle that has been in a 21°C room can be put somewhere cool (the fridge, or outside in cold weather) for, say, 15–20 minutes depending on the temperature.

Joanna Simon
Wine writer, Sunday Times

A QUICK FLICK

If there are little bits of cork floating in the neck of a bottle of wine when you have opened it, get rid of them by holding the bottle firmly at the bottom, tilting it a bit and with a short, sharp, sideways flick of the wrist the pieces of cork, not the wine, will fall into the sink. It takes practice but it isn't difficult.

Martin Bredda
Chef to Mr David and Lady Pamela Hicks

TWO-WAY WINNER

Always decant cheap wine and leave old, good wine in the bottle. Young, cheap wine is improved by decanting and a further advantage lies in the fact that the guest can see the bottle and read the label of your best wine and will probably be perfectly happy with whatever is in the decanter.

The Hon. W. S. Pease

FILL 'EM UP

If you are left with two or more half-full bottles of wine after a party, mix them together to get full bottles to restopper: they will keep better than air-filled half-empty bottles. Keep them in a cool place and drink over the next day or two. The wines need to be the same colour but otherwise you shouldn't have any qualms about mixing claret with Chianti or Australian Chardonnay with South African Sauvignon. You might come up with a great blend.

Joanna Simon
Wine writer, Sunday Times

MULL IT OVER

For a nice easy-to-make mulled wine, perfect for a cold winter's night, wash 6 tangerines and stick 2 cloves in each. Put them in a large pan with 2 cinnamon sticks, 2 bottles of French country red wine, 2 glasses of brandy and sugar to taste. Heat gently to just below boiling and serve warm.

Mrs H. Brunton

PRECAUTION

When contemplating a night's heavy drinking, don't wait until the next day for a hangover cure. Eat two slices of toast and peanut butter before you start drinking and then drink equal quantities of fizzy water to alcohol.

Kathleen Griffin
Food writer

BEETHOVEN'S FIFTH

A measure each of crème de cassis and peach schnapps in a flute (non-musical) topped up with champagne, *poco agitato*. Heavenly music.

Steve Race
Radio musical-quiz master

POUSSE-CAFÉ

Flatter chauvinistic French guests with a tricolour pousse-café made by carefully pouring equal quantities of grenadine, Cointreau and Bols blue liqueur into suitable glasses such as flutes so that they remain separated from each other to give a red, white and blue effect. Another version gives a rainbow effect. Carefully pour in the following order equal portions of grenadine, maraschino, red curaçao, yellow Chartreuse and top with fine brandy.

Alan Root

THE PERFECT MARTINI

Though it is now somewhat out of fashion, the dry Martini remains the king of cocktails. If you want to produce the king of dry Martinis, subtly and indefinably different from all others, add one drop (not more) of ouzo or raki to each glass after it has been poured and before adding the indispensable zest of lemon peel. Avoid onions and olives at all costs.

John Julius Norwich
Author and broadcaster

NAUGHTY

One of my favourite, and perhaps most wicked, tips is telling friends to be sure to put their bottles of vodka in the freezer as it makes it wonderfully syrupy.

Deborah Owen
Literary agent

WHAT THE BUTLER MADE

This is my grandfather's butler's recipe for a Christmas party drink. First, marinate 2 handfuls of raisins overnight. Then add 1 bottle non-vintage port, 1¼ bottles gin, ½ bottle brandy, a carton of orange juice, a handful of flaked almonds, some sticks of cinnamon, grated nutmeg, cloves and a 1 lb (450 g) packet of soft brown sugar. Add a large pot of Indian tea to dilute and serve hot. This will do twenty-two people exceedingly well.

Roddy Llewellyn
Garden designer and landscaper

BLOODY GOOD

The smoothest and most delicious Bloody Mary is made in a large tumbler with two inches vodka, two inches sherry, the juice of half a lemon, one dessertspoon horseradish sauce, six big splashes of Worcestershire sauce and Tabasco and one teaspoon piled with salt. Fill the remaining inch and a half of the tumbler with tomato juice.

Nicholas Coleridge
Managing Director, Condé Nast

SIMPLY SWEETER

Always keep a bottle of sugar syrup (made by dissolving 1½ lb (675 g) of sugar in 1 pt (600 ml) of water and boiling for five minutes) in the fridge. It helps to make wonderful cocktails. A whisky sour, for instance, tastes much better with this than if just sugar has been added.

Germain Schwab
Patron, Winteringham Fields, South Humberside

REVIVING

When everything seems to be getting on top of you, make an egg flip. Beat a teaspoonful of sugar into the yolk of an egg, heat 10 fl oz (300 ml) milk and whisk that into the egg mixture. While this is cooling, whisk an egg white and fold it, with a tablespoon of sherry or brandy, into the milk. Serve in a tumbler.

Tony Baldry MP

CHEAT'S PIMMS

I may not have rumbled Pimms' secret recipe, but this is a delicious substitute. Take one measure of gin, one measure of red vermouth (French or Italian) and half a measure of orange curaçao. Fill up with fizzy lemonade and ice and add a slice each of lemon, orange and cucumber in the usual way.

Jane MacQuitty
The Times *Wine Correspondent*

A FRUITIER FLAVOUR

Try frozen strawberries and raspberries in Pimms' instead of ice-cubes. They won't dilute the drink as they thaw; they'll give it extra flavour.

Mike Page
Merchant banker

FORTY FORTE

The strength of this delicious orange gin depends on the strength of the gin you use to make it. The choice is yours. Push 40 peppercorns into the skin of a large orange and put it in a wide-necked jar (I use a 5 pt (3-litre) kilner jar). Add 40 lumps of sugar and fill it up with gin. Seal and leave it for 40 days, giving the jar a shake whenever you remember. Decant into bottles and drink with caution.

Alexander Petrie
Undergraduate

EXACTITUDE

There are various recipes for sloe gin but I have implicit belief in the importance of accurate measuring – you must have *equal* weight of sloes and sugar filled to *half-way* up the bottle. And I don't believe the old theory about waiting for the frost to soften the sloes – they've usually been eaten by birds by then. Far better to pick them black and blooming and prick the skins.

Mary Goldring
Freelance economist

QUICK PRICK SLOE

I'm afraid I don't have the patience to prick each sloe when I make sloe gin. I pick the fruit before the birds have feasted and put it in the freezer. When the sloes thaw, having been frozen, their skins conveniently burst and pricking is unnecessary.

Sophie Page

FLOWERS IN ICE

For a showy after-dinner treat, decant a bottle of kümmel or Cointreau into a clear glass bottle and put it into a cylindrical container slightly too large for it up to its shoulders. Pour water into the container round the bottle mixed with whatever wild flowers you fancy and put it in the deep freeze. When you take it out of the freezer, rinse under the hot tap to release the container and you will slide out your spectacular iced flowery bottle.

Gervase Jackson-Stops

COOLER

For a really refreshing drink on a hot summer's day, try a mint cooler. Make some sugar syrup and pour it, while still hot, over mint leaves and add some lemon juice. Cover and steep it for an hour, strain it, add grape juice to taste and put it in the fridge. Before serving, add ginger ale to taste.

Monica Bannister

JET LIFT

When I want a delicious soft drink I squeeze the juice of a whole lemon into a tumbler of de-fizzed Diet Coca-Cola, which is wonderfully refreshing, especially on a long jet flight. But I always take lemons with me as airlines only seem to carry slices, which are impossible to squeeze.

David Hicks
Interior and garden designer

BRIGHTER WITH BITTERS

Fizzy water or tonic can be much enlivened by a dash of Angostura bitters.

Andrea Newman
Writer

ORANGE BLOSSOM DRINK

Make a very soothing drink by adding a few drops of orange blossom essence (you can buy it in Indian or Middle Eastern grocers) to boiling water. Try it before you go to bed; it is supposed to give you sweet dreams.

Claudia Roden
Food writer

COLD HANDS I LOVE

For really cold drinks on a hot summer day, put the glasses in the deep freeze to frost them.

Lucinda Green
Three-day eventer

LEMON CUBES

Squeeze lemons or limes and freeze the juice in ice-cube trays. A delicious way to drink water is by putting one or two of these cubes in each glass.

Marchioness of Tavistock

QUICK PICK-ME-UP

Put half a banana, a teaspoonful of sugar and 10 fl oz (300 ml) milk into the food processor. When you have consumed it you will feel ready for anything, no matter how tired you were before.

Revd Barbara Clement

CURE (NEARLY) ALL

For a possible cure for arthritis and rheumatic infections – and a good drink anyway – squeeze 3 oranges, 3 lemons and 3 grapefruit. Set the juice aside and put all the skins, seeds and pulp through the mixer and cover with 2 pt (1.25 litres) of boiling water. Add the fruit juices and allow to stand over night. Next day strain carefully, dissolve 2 oz (50 g) of cream of tartar and 2 oz (50 g) of Epsom salts in 1 pt (600 ml) of boiling water and add to the juice. Bottle, stir well and take one port-wine-size glass every morning before breakfast.

Douglas Cobham

141

ICED COFFEE

Make some extra coffee at breakfast and keep it in the fridge. When you want iced coffee, put this in the blender with an ice-cube per person plus milk and sugar. Blend to a creamy consistency and drink through a straw.

Bamber Gascoigne
Author and TV presenter

FRESH GROUND

In order to have perfectly fresh-roasted coffee beans whenever you want, lob the beans straight into a plastic box and put them in the freezer. Scoop out as required and grind them frozen.

Ian Carmichael
Actor

NOT BITTER, BETTER

The only good way to make coffee is the plunge method in a cafetière. Use any good ground coffee and be sure to pour a good dose of boiling water on to the coffee before you plunge. And, always pour boiling water over the *plunger* before plunging it into the coffee. Serve as soon as possible. Coffee should taste as good as it smells and the smell soon disappears. Never leave it to brew, as that makes it bitter.

Sir Hardy Amies
Designer

TAKE CARE

Take care not to be too forceful when pushing down the coffee plunger. It can happen – and I have seen it – that the glass will burst, with horrifying results!

Christopher Leland
Farmer

GETTING BETTER

Instant coffee can never be the 'real thing' but it gets noticeably nearer to it if a little brandy is added during the making.

Maggie Black
Food historian

AROMA

A couple of ground cardamon pods added to the cafetière gives you the most wonderfully perfumed coffee as drunk in Southern India.

Christopher Gable
Artistic Director, Northern Ballet Theatre

TEA TIME

Freeze cubes of well-flavoured tea (Ceylon, Earl Grey, etc.) and cubes of minted lemon juice and water. Add these to cold drinks of apple juice, cider or spa water to make delicious iced tea.

Jean Alexander
Catering Manager, Forest Mere, Liphook

OLD-FASHIONED

If you like to drink your China tea with sugar and lemon, try dissolving an old-fashioned lemon drop in it instead. It's lovely.

Kathy O'Shea
Hair stylist

HEALTHY EATING AND LOSING WEIGHT

Bachelor's fare: bread and cheese and kisses.

Jonathan Swift

WEIGHT WATCHING

When I want to lose weight, I stick a really awful fat-looking photograph of myself on the fridge and I don't take it down until I've got back to the right size.

Prue Leith
Food writer and restaurateur

BUTTON UP

If you want to lose weight fast without getting tired, eat nothing but a 4 oz (100 g) steak and a grilled tomato for lunch and supper for two or three days. By then most of your buttons will do up.

Janet Suzman
Actress

LESS FAT

One very good way of reducing fat intake is a mistake I made myself making soup. I boiled the vegetables first, forgetting to sauté them in butter. When liquidizing I did add some butter – but nothing like as much as I would have used had I fried them first. This produced a wonderful emulsified soup.

Julia, Lady de Saumarez
Proprietor, Shrubland Clinic, Coddenham

TOOTHSOME

Always clean your teeth immediately after meals. The astringent taste of the toothpaste will stop any desire to pick at left-overs and your teeth will benefit as well as your waistline.

Lady Cazalet

TITBIT DIET

Always keep a stock of crudités (raw carrot, celery, fennel, cauliflower, red, green and yellow peppers) cut into bite-sized batons in the fridge. Offer them instead of salted peanuts – which are very fattening – with aperitifs. Best of all, eat them while you prepare a meal: they'll take the edge off your appetite and keep your waistline out of the Guinness book of records.

Lynda Brown
Food writer

LIGHTER

Adding *crème fraîche* to a sauce instead of ordinary cream will make it lighter.

Keith Marshall
Chef and Proprietor, The Dew Pond, Old Burghclere

PEPPERED PUDDING

My husband, who is very much aware of his need to diet, does a lot of business-class flying. He has worked out a brilliant way to stop himself eating the pudding bit of his in-flight meal. Whilst his will power is still strong enough, he opens the pepper and shakes it all over his gateau or whatever. He then eats up the rest while the man beside him worries about his sanity.

Mrs John Joint

SLIMMERS' ALTERNATIVE

If a recipe calls for sour cream replace it with low-fat yoghurt: much kinder to your scales.

Peggy Osher

HIGH FIBRE, LOW FAT

High fibre foods, such as pasta, wholemeal bread, potatoes and pulses also tend to be low in fat and are a valuable source of vitamins and minerals and starchy carbohydrate. Together with fruit and vegetables, they fill you up and do you good.

Trevor Hancock
Chef, Henlow Grange and Hydro Springs Hydro

CHALLENGED?

If all the excitement, a couple of years ago, about the cholesterol-lowering effect of oats caused you to switch to an oat breakfast cereal and this has caused you to be – how can we put it nicely, posterially challenged? – switch back to All Bran, or the own-brand supermarket look-alikes or any wheat-based cereal with at least 20 per cent dietary fibre.

Audrey Eyton
Author of The F-Plan Diet

GIVE IT A SQUEEZE

Rather than making a syrup to go over a fruit salad, with all the attendant calories, I use freshly squeezed orange juice.

Jan Leeming
TV presenter

COUNT DOWN

When making a fruit salad, instead of using a syrup to soak the fruit in, use low-calorie lemonade. It will prevent the fruit from browning and reduce the calories.

Dr Eileen Barratt
Nutritionist, Inglewood Health Hydro, Kintbury

OIL FREE

It is possible to make a vinaigrette dressing without oil – a boon to the seriously committed dieter. Whisk together 1½ fl oz (45 ml) white wine vinegar, 2½ fl oz (75 ml) water, 1 teaspoon each of Dijon mustard and clear honey, ½ teaspoon freshly chopped chervil and some freshly ground black pepper. Store it in a sealed container in the fridge and use as required.

Paul Spink
Head Chef, Ragdale Hall, Melton Mowbray

TRELLIS WORK

If you are, as I am, a lover of food wrapped in, or topped with pastry, but do not want a heavy meal, a trellis cutter is the ideal piece of equipment for you. With this instrument you will need approximately a quarter of the pastry to get the same effect.

Anton Edelmann
Maître Chef des Cuisines, The Savoy, London

WATER

Keep a jug of water in the fridge with two or three slices of lemon in it. Cheaper and nicer than bottled water and very good for those on a diet who are trying to drink lots of water every day.

The Marchioness of Zetland

COCONUT MILK

Cooking for people who are allergic to dairy products can be a problem, especially when making something which needs milk, such as a white sauce or a rice pudding. Coconut milk, which now, thank goodness, comes in tins and can be found on the supermarket shelves, is a perfect substitute.

Sara Allday
Colour counsellor

BINDINGS

For those who may not use eggs or have none to hand, I find that plain yoghurt is a good binding agent. Similarly, when coating rissoles or fish with breadcrumbs, milk is almost as good as egg for the 'undercoat'.

Dame Beryl Grey
Prima ballerina

NOT SO BAD

I am one of the oldies who has, for health reasons, to subsist on a fat-free diet – that is, a diet as free from animal fat as possible. No bread-and-butter, but bread-and-marg, which sounds dreadful, a real Dotheboys Hall diet. But it isn't. Toast or bread can be delicious if it is spread with soya margarine. It even has a slight buttery flavour.

Elizabeth Longford
Author

IN THE DEEP FREEZE

The ice was here, the ice was there,
The ice was all around.
It cracked and growled, and roared and howled,
Like noises in a swound.

SAMUEL TAYLOR COLERIDGE

AIDE MEMOIRE

Keep a permanent marker Pentel pen (N50) and a roll of masking tape in the kitchen drawer. The pen will write on plastic bags or on strips of the tape to stick on plastic boxes for the fridge or freezer. Contents, details and instructions such as 'your dinner' or 'cat's dinner' can be quickly stuck on and easily removed when finished.

Nicola Cox
Food writer and demonstrator

... The secret of a happy life in the kitchen is clear labelling. Buy a large quantity of jam-pot labels and identify all dubious edibles in cupboards and the freezer. This will avoid the 'I knew this would come in useful one day, but I'm not sure what it is' scenario when faced with green frozen liquid lurking in the freezer drawer.

Kathleen Griffin
Food writer

... Give a different colour to each category of food and package the food in coloured bags, or use coloured ties, so that you can see at a glance where fish, meat etc. is.

I find a freezer record book makes heavy weather of freezing. Instead, I use a large wipe-off board on the kitchen wall. As packs are put in, I record them; as packs are taken out I wipe them off. In this way I know exactly what's there. I also write the engineer's number up there in case of an emergency.

Mary Berry
Food writer, broadcaster and TV demonstrator

BEWARE THE FLUFF

Take care to wrap everything before it goes in the freezer. Not only will it keep better, but if like me, you put your mohair sweaters to freeze for twelve hours to stop them moulting, you'll keep your food fluff-free. I do, of course, put the jumper in a bag as well.

Rabbi Julia Neuberger

RUNNY HONEY

Store a honeycomb in the freezer to prevent it

from solidifying. This may sound improbable but it does thaw out runny.

The Lady Carrington

SNOW WHITE

If you don't want apples to go brown when you freeze them, here's the answer. Peel and core them in the usual way and submerge them immediately in salty water. Dry them in a clean towel, bag them up and pop them in the freezer.

Baroness Blatch

FOILED

If you are short of freezer containers for casseroles etc. line any suitable dish with a large piece of foil, pour in the cooked stew or whatever, fold the foil over the top and freeze. Then you can lift out the packet and re-use the dish.

The Hon. Lady Butler

READY FOR BABY

Vegetables prepared for adult meals can be sieved, put into ice-cube trays and frozen. They then provide flexible amounts of food for babies beginning to take solids.

The Lady Tombs

THE MORE THE MERRIER

It is just as easy and nearly as quick to make a large amount of risotto as a little, and it freezes extremely well. Next time you make some, make extra and freeze the rest.

Mrs Cherry Large
Katharine House Hospice voluntary helper

NOT TOO MUCH, NOT TOO LITTLE

It can be tricky to defrost the right amount of soup for a given number of people. Solve the problem by putting polythene bags in the bowls from which the soup is to be served, pour the soup to be frozen to the required level and freeze. Take the bags out of the soup bowls when they are frozen and keep together in large polythene bags until needed.

Ruth Watson
Chef and Proprietor, The Fox and Goose Inn, Fressingfield

GIVE IT SPACE

When freezing most things it is sensible to remove excess air. This is fatal with rice or grated cheese. With these, leave plenty of room in the bag and after the initial freeze, shake and rearrange the contents into separate grains.

The Countess of Minto

AT THE READY

I think everyone knows that sliced bread can be used straight from the freezer. But I like to keep a large bag of breadcrumbs and a bag of grated cheese there as well. Both can be shaken out and used immediately when a recipe calls for a small amount of either.

The Hon. Lady Butler

WINE CUBES

Any wine that is left over after a dinner party (even in people's glasses but don't tell anyone) can be poured into ice trays to freeze. Bag the cubes up and use them in stews and soups as required at a later date.

Mrs Roddy Llewellyn

SAVE FOR STOCK

Freeze bones for stock until you have enough to make it worthwhile boiling up a large panful. Once stock is made, strained and the fat removed, boil it until it is reduced to a concentrated 'glacé'. Freeze it in cubes. When you come to use it just add water to return the stock to its desired strength.

Sophie Grigson
Food writer

PEG IT

The half-finished bag of vegetables in the freezer: don't faff with those prissy little ties – just clip it together with a clothes-peg.

Katharine Whitehorn
Journalist

SPARE PARTS

It is unlikely that you will want to make meringues at the same time as you have spare egg whites. So put them in ice-cube trays. Once frozen they can be tipped into a bag. They will keep for six months in the freezer and will still be whippable if they are thawed slowly in the refrigerator.

Richard Baker
Broadcaster and author

NOT UP TO SCRATCH

Do you, like me, end up with tattered knuckles every time you prepare grated lemon rind? Now, after squeezing the juice from halved lemons, I pop the rinds in the freezer wrapped in plastic. When the rinds are frozen hard it is easy to grate them and obtain a fine zest.

Jackie Franks

SAVE THE END

When cutting up lemons to get slices for your gin and tonic, don't throw away the ends but put them in a polythene bag in the deep freeze ready for making marmalade.

Miranda Hall
Cordon bleu demonstrator

CHILL OUT

When making ice-cream or sorbet, or indeed anything that you want to chill quickly, put a metal spoon into the mixture while it is freezing. The metal conducts the cold down into the mixture, thereby speeding the chilling process.

Nikki Kowan-Kedge
*Restaurateur, The Loaves and Fishes Restaurant,
Marlborough*

EASY TURN OUT

Take your ice tray out of the freezer half an hour before the ice is needed. Keep it at room temperature and the cubes will turn out easily and whole. For a party, collect ice-cubes and put them in opaque white plastic bags in the freezer – then they won't stick together.

Gail Bredda
Housekeeper to Mr David and Lady Pamela Hicks

FAST ICE

It seems logical to fill an ice tray with cold water, but if in fact you fill it with hot the ice will form far quicker. It works on the simple principle of evaporation.

David Emmanuel
Designer

NO SPILLS

Place ice-cube containers on a plastic tray in the freezer. This will avoid continual spillage which creates an arctic scene of ice lumps which make for more spillage.

Jennifer Paterson
Food writer

CRUSHED

This is a really quick way to have almost instant crushed ice. Run cold water into a freezer bag (choose a big one), then knot it tightly. Lie the bag on a baking sheet so that the water runs into a thin layer. Then freeze the tray and the bag. To crush the ice, drop the bag on the floor once or twice, then tip out the ice and use.

Katie Stewart
Food writer

DEFROST

Use a hair-drier to defrost the freezer – this considerably speeds up the process.

Claire Neilson

BREAKDOWN

In the event of a freezer breakdown, cover it with layers of overcoats, eiderdowns, duvets, etc. to delay thawing. Fill any empty spaces in the interior with cardboard boxes or crumpled newspaper to lessen the air content. If the breakdown is long-lasting, cook any frozen foods which have thawed and hope the freezer will have recovered in time to freeze them again.

Derek Bell

THE WELL-EQUIPPED COOK

Give us the tools and we'll finish the job.

SIR WINSTON CHURCHILL

BROWNED OFF

Caramelizing a *crème brûlée* is really impossible under an electric grill and very difficult under a gas one. But now it is possible to buy, at your local DIY store, little blowtorches, fired with small gas cylinders, with which it is simple to run a flame over the pudding, caramelizing the sugar without cooking the custard.

Patrick McDonald
Chef and Proprietor, Epicurian, Cheltenham

BLOW OUT

Always have a little blowtorch in the kitchen. Then, when you want to turn out a mousse, chocolate slice or ice-cream, use it to go round the sides of the tin: it will heat the puddings just enough to slide out easily. And when you come to cut them, use the blowtorch to heat the knife – a hot blade slices more efficiently.

Charles Whittaker
Chef and Proprietor, Country Friends Restaurant,
Dorrington

HOT AIR

I used to hate unmoulding a mousse. A dip in hot water often melted the whole thing; or with the shake-on-the-plate method only half of it would come away. Now I turn it upside-down on to the serving plate and give it a quick blow with a hair-drier.

Jilly Cooper
Writer

LUMP IT

As most silver teapots are brought out for special occasions and not used regularly, it is a good idea to keep a lump of sugar in the pot while it is put away. Remember to take it out when you make the tea, though.

Sam Twining
Tea merchant

COLD COMFORT

Are you fed up with your cling film not tearing properly and sticking together? Keep it in the fridge and it will behave impeccably.

Mrs S. Foyster

SAVINGS

Keep old butter wrappers in the fridge to grease soufflé dishes or line cake tins.

Madge Bridges
Actress

PERFECT TIMING

When one is trying to cook a special meal and the telephone keeps ringing, and one is besieged with callers, a good timer with a loud 'ping' is essential.

Eric Loderer
Chef and Proprietor, Manleys, Storrington

SEE-THROUGH SURFACE

A ¼-in (0.6-cm) thick sheet of glass turns any old table into a superb working surface, hygienic, easy to clean etc. Just remember not to put hot saucepans on it.

Mary Goldring
Freelance economist

BUG FREE

Why have butchers always used wooden chopping blocks? Because for some reason known to scientists but not to me, bacteria that affect meat will not grow in wood. So carry on using that battered old wooden board and resist the charms of the flash-looking plastic ones.

Richard Good
Merchant banker

BIN IT

Cover your chopping board with newspaper and peel, chop, etc. the vegetables and fruit on top of that. Then, when the whole job's finished, fold up the paper around the debris and chuck it all away.

Mrs Julian Fellowes

SOFT AS BUTTER

If you need soft butter and all you have is hard from the fridge or even the freezer, grate it. And sprinkle a little flour on the grater to stop it sticking.

Barbara Bartlett

SAY CHEESE

If you hold the cheese grater under the cold tap before using it, the cheese won't stick to it and it will be easier to wash.

Lady Cazalet

GINGER GRATER

I broke my garlic press trying to crush ginger in it and now my favourite new gadget is a bamboo ginger grater, available from increasingly widespread oriental stockists. You rub the peeled ginger on serrated soft-wood slats, which remove all the pulp and juice and leave you holding a bunch of bristly fibres.

Rosemary Stark
Food writer

NO WASHING-UP

I hate washing up the grill pan. Now I never have to. I always line it with foil so that all I have to do is scrunch up the lining and throw it away when the cooking is done.

Mary Roberts
Secretary, Katharine House Hospice

PANCAKE PAN

Keep a special pan just for pancakes. When it is new, season by filling with vegetable oil and a little salt, leaving it for twenty-four hours and wiping it clean with a cloth or kitchen paper. After that, never wash it with detergent; just wipe it carefully after each use.

Elisabeth Collett
Food studies lecturer

A KINDER CUT

A really big sharp knife – one that can be resharpened easily and regularly – is an essential piece of equipment. Not only is it much more satisfying to use: it doesn't damage the fibre of the food. All sorts of meat, fish and vegetables can have flavour as well as appearance damaged by hand-to-hand combat with a blunt knife. And fate also dictates that guests will walk into the kitchen just as the damaged piece of meat is being catapulted across the kitchen floor towards the cat!

Nick Mason
Drummer with Pink Floyd and food enthusiast

… If you want to buy a really sharp knife, go to a second-hand shop and purchase one with an old steel blade. It won't be as smart and shiny as a stainless-steel one but you will be able to keep it razor-sharp with any sort of sharpener.

Christopher Leland
Farmer

CUT OUT THE SMELL

It sounds – and looks – crazy, but if your kitchen

knives persistently smell of meat or onions, plunge them into the earth (garden or window-box) several times. Wash well afterwards, of course.

Mary Berry
Cookery writer, broadcaster and TV demonstrator

SHOWER CAPS

Good hotels are usually very generous with the goodies they provide in the bathroom – bath stuff, shampoo and so on. I go for the shower caps and stash one away in my suitcase every day. They make perfect covers for bowls of left-overs etc. in the fridge.

Joan Bakewell
Actress

TELL TAILS

To find things instantly in a heaped-up kitchen drawer, make coloured tails for whatever you use most. My potato peeler has a tail of red string, and my favourite knife sports pipe cleaners.

The Lady Saye and Sele

POST IT

Our dustbin stands outside the wall of our kitchen and we have had a large 'letter box' let into the wall above the bin with a chute going down into it. We tie the neck of the dustbin liner round the end of the chute and post our rubbish out of the kitchen straight into the bin. We have a flap on the 'letter box' to stop nasty smells wafting back into the kitchen.

The Lady Wardington

HIT FOR SIX

I keep one of my old cricket bats in the kitchen because it is the perfect piece of equipment for bashing an escalope of veal really flat.

Sir Colin Cowdray

COOL IT

If you want to cool a pot of stock etc. quickly, rest the pan on a spoon to allow circulation of air underneath.

James Graham
Chef and Proprietor, Ostlers Close, Cupar

FATLESS

A sheet of kitchen paper between two round sieves will blot the fat off soup and sauces quickly and easily.

Jean Alexander
Catering Manager, Forest Mere, Liphook

GETTING UP STEAM

If you have to wear glasses in the kitchen and you find they steam up, heat them up by dipping them in hot water. The same holds for reading in the bath.

The Lady May

… You can prevent spectacles from steaming up whilst working in the kitchen by wiping the lenses with washing-up liquid, then polishing them off with a soft cloth.

HRH The Duchess of York

DRIPLESS

Smooth a little butter under the lip of a milk or

cream jug – this will prevent drips.

The Lady Grantley

NO OVERFLOW

If, like me, when boiling milk you forget all about it, try smoothing a little butter on the inside rim of the saucepan. This should stop it boiling over.

Emily Perry
Actress

A GOOD GRIP

When first opening a jar, wear a rubber glove on the hand you use to turn the lid. This will give you a far better grip and the jar should open easily.

Christine Hancock
General Secretary, Royal College of Nursing

… If you have difficulty getting the lid off a jam jar, invert the jar and place it on the hot plate of the Aga for a few seconds. It will then turn easily.

Miranda Hall
Cordon bleu demonstrator

STINK OUT

Spilt milk or cream can leave the most ghastly smell, especially on fabric. Rubbing the affected area with a strong solution of bicarbonate of soda and water will solve the problem.

Lady Macdonald of Macdonald
Cookery writer

STAINS

Salt will remove beet stains from wet hands. Rub well and wash with soap and water.

Patricia Lousada
Food writer

BLOCKED PIPES

Never throw egg shells down the waste-disposal unit. They grind away to coat your pipes with an irremovable cement-like lining which will eventually block them completely.

Ray Cherry
Master builder

PENNY WISE

It is worth knowing that a 20p coin weighs exactly 5 g (three 20p coins weigh ½ oz). If you use pan scales and lose a small weight the coin will do the trick – and if you doubt the accuracy of your electronic scales you can weigh one to check them.

Richard Bishop
Head of the Coin and Medal dept., Christie's

SCALED DOWN

When the ingredients of a recipe are to be added gradually to a saucepan or bowl, place the pan or bowl on the scales first and note the weight. Then add the various items while the pan is sitting on the scales.

Patrick Anthony
TV cook

DON'T FORGET

When faced with left-over egg whites – or yolks – all ideas for using them suddenly seem to evaporate. Solve this by pinning *aide-mémoires* to your kitchen noticeboard: one listing favourite recipes and cooking techniques which call for more white than yolks, such as cheese soufflé, apple snow or clarifying consommé; another listing things that major on egg yolks, like Scotch woodcock, mayonnaise, glazing puff pastry and brioche dough. Keep on adding to the lists.

Philippa Davenport
Food and cookery writer, Financial Times *and* Country Living

MAKE A RECORD

It is a good idea to keep an index book for recording recipes that you have tried and liked. Simply list the name of the dish under headings such as 'Fish', 'Puddings' or whatever, and the cookery book it came from with the appropriate page number. This can save hours of hunting through your cookery books for something you made but can't remember where it came from.

Elizabeth Jane Howard
Author

COLOURED-CODED

Use different-coloured index cards, or coloured index labels in books, for various types of recipes. For instance, green for vegetable dishes, red for meat, white for chicken, etc.

Y. *Christie*

CUPBOARD LOVE

Stick often-needed recipes inside the door of the kitchen cupboard for quick and easy reference.

Myrtle Allen
Chef and Proprietor, Ballymaloe House, County Cork

CLEARING UP
AFTERWARDS

C-l-e-a-n, clean, verb active, to make brighter, to scour. W-i-n, win, d-e-r, der, winder, a casement.

CHARLES DICKENS

DEVOTION

I *like* washing-up. By hand, no machines, to the dismay of my more advanced children. I wear yellow gloves and plod through the previous night's detritus. I recommend a splash of ammonia in the bowl – it *does* cut the grease and the peculiar smell grows on you, if, like me, you are committed to the chore. By the way, the only other keen washer-uppers I know are all men. What does that tell us?

Jocasta Innes
Food writer

THE HANDS THAT WASH DISHES …

When washing up, *always* wear gloves.

Fiona Fullerton
Actress

SPARKLERS

Sometimes it is better to wash glasses by hand than put them in the dishwasher. In which case, for pristine results you will need a bowl of really hot water, Fairy Liquid and a large lemon. If you have two bowls squeeze the lemon into the rinsing water; if not it works just as well with the washing-up liquid. Wash the glasses and drain them upside-down on a warm tea-towel. They dry very quickly, with barely a watermark, and buff up beautifully.

Rt. Hon. Baroness Chalker of Wallasey

AS IF BY MAGIC

To make your drinking glasses gleam, hold them over the steam of a kettle and polish up with a paper kitchen towel.

Paul Daniels
Magician

BOTTOMS UP

Always put cutlery into the dishwasher with the 'working' ends up. They need the swirling water to clean them whereas the handles are presumably quite clean.

Barbara Cochrane

MOVE ALONG

If you are holding an informal party with finger buffet and drinks, at which guests will be arriving at irregular intervals, don't try to keep pace with the washing-up. Simply pile all the dirty crockery and cutlery on one side of the sink and all the dirty glasses on the other. Then, in the morning – move.

John Junkin
Actor

CLEAN DECANTERS

An easy way to clean wine decanters is to add a little rice to some hot soapy water, leave them to soak and rinse clean.

Robert Lyons
Resident Director, The Bay Horse Inn, Ulverston

… The way to get the gunk out of the bottom of oddly shaped vases or decanters is not to muck about with lead shot and all that; simply pour in some of the stuff people use for their dentures, Steradent and such.

Katharine Whitehorn
Journalist

… We clean the inside of a decanter with hand-hot salt water and rinse with clear water. The easiest way to dry the inside is to fill it with hot water and hold it upside-down under the cold water tap allowing the hot water to drain away. Miraculously, the inside will be dry and dripless.

P. J. Welsh
Director, Tyringham Naturopathic Clinic,
Newport Pagnell

NO REMINDERS

My abiding memory of picnics in my childhood was the tea from the thermos which always smelt of the soup we had had in it the time before. Now I know that if I wash the thing out, dry it well, put salt in it and screw the lid on, it will be fresh with no reminiscences.

Rosemary Jenkins
Director of Professional Affairs to the
Royal College of Midwives

TEA TIME

Tea is susceptible to smell, so it is as wrong to put detergent in the teapot as it is wrong to put the teapot in the dishwasher. You should rinse the pot out with cold water after use, and should you need to clean it, place 2 teaspoonfuls of bicarbonate of soda (USA baking powder) in the pot, pour in boiling water and leave for 2 or 3 hours.

If you have sinned and used detergent, the best way to sweeten it again is to leave some dry tea leaves in the pot for a few days.

Sam Twining
Tea merchant

A WAY WITH WAX

If your silver candleholders are coated with wax, place them in the freezer for an hour or so. The wax will peel off in a jiffy with absolutely no injury to the silver.

Lady Otton

HIGH AND DRY

After washing and drying piping bags, hang them in a warm place, perhaps over the stove, and after an hour or so they will be as dry as a bone and also bacteria-free.

Marc Preston
Chef and Proprietor, La Fleur de Lys Restaurant, Shaftesbury

SWEET SMELLING

When you're cleaning the oven, put a glassful of vinegar in the rinsing water. It will neutralize whatever property it is in the cleaner that makes it smell so unpleasant.

Mrs Michael Aspel

SQUEEZY CLEAN

If you've got a ceramic hob, the easiest way to keep it clean is to rub it over when it is cool with half a lemon – an already-squeezed one will do. A final wipe with a bit of kitchen paper and it will be as new.

Barbara Bartlett

EFFORTLESS

There is nothing more frustrating and time-consuming than trying to remove stuck-on food – particularly scrambled eggs – from the bottom of a pan. But if you sprinkle a small amount of dishwasher powder into it, pour on boiling water and leave it to soak for an hour or until the food is loosened – hey presto! Clean pan and no effort. Stained teacups etc. also enjoy this treatment.

Andrée L. Massey
The Icing Parlour, York

BURN OFF

When a saucepan has been burnt, instantly boil a cupful of malt vinegar and water in it for about ten minutes. It usually does the trick.

Mrs John Hawkesworth

BRIGHT AS NEW

A discoloured saucepan can be returned to its original shine if you boil water in it with a teaspoon of cream of tartar and leave it for ten minutes.

S. Cullum

THE OLD-FASHIONED WAY

A silver-cleaning cloth should always be to hand,

and here's a nice old-fashioned way to make your own. Mix together 1 tablespoon of Goddard's silver powder, 3 tablespoons of methylated spirits and a gallon of water. Put a towel to soak in the mixture overnight, lift it out dripping and dry it where it won't make a mess. When dry, shake it well (breathing out, if possible!). It will last for ages.

Moira Shearer
Ballerina and author

WRAP IT UP

If you wrap silver in cling film after it has been cleaned, it will be protected from tarnishing.

Mrs J. E. H. Collins

THE ANSWER'S A LEMON

Clean a copper bowl by sprinkling it with salt and scrubbing with half a lemon. If a copper saucepan is particularly dirty and burnt, a mixture of tomato sauce and lemon will clean off the burnt areas and make the saucepan shine.

Pamela, Lady Harlech

SAUCY

From schoolday jobs as hall porter in country hotels, I learned two things about making dull surfaces shine. Use HP Sauce on brass knobs and knockers and concentrated orange squash on ceramic tiles.

Tom Jaine
Editor, Good Food Guide

FOR THOSE WHO DON'T COOK

*Heaven sends us good meat; but the Devil
sends cooks.*

DAVID GARRICK

NO-GO AREA

One should avoid the kitchen and its fall-out area
at all times. Employ a young, bright female cook
who will be induced by your flattery to stay for
years, and train your children at an early age to
load the dishwasher and clear up after Dad who
has used every pan in sight, and more, on cook's
day off.

Lady Montagu of Beaulieu

EAT OUT

My husband describes my cookery as Cordon
Noire. In our house the dustbin has ulcers, we pray

172

after we've eaten and the dog begs for Rennies. Therefore my best hint is to eat out as often as possible or give Meals-on-Wheels an annual contract.

Rachel Heyhoe Flint
Cricketer, journalist and broadcaster

WELL MADE

The best thing for a tired working woman to make is a reservation for dinner at her favourite restaurant.

Claire Rayner
Agony aunt

SUPPERS ONLY

I belong to the group of people who find cooking a tedious, generally unrewarding business, unless it is all being done by someone else, and consider recipe swapping about as alluring as the sight of washing-up. So I offer supper to my guests instead of dinner, so no one expects me to think up amusing starters or agonize over the syllabub.

Frankie McGowan
Journalist

TAKE THE CAKE

If you're serving wedges of gateau for a party or a coffee morning don't sweat over the hot stove. Get your local baker to make you a catering block, from which you'll get 20–30 pieces. I order mine in advance and collect it, oozing with fresh cream, at 7.30 a.m., in time for my charity coffee mornings. Delicious, and no trouble at all – except for the cream in the boot of the car.

Mrs Edwina Currie MP

ENJOY

When it comes to cooking, know your limitations and enjoy the offering of others – and *show* that you enjoy.

Ronald Pickup
Actor

BAD BOY

As one whose cookery skills go just about as far as removing the lids from yoghurt tubs efficiently, my hint for husbands who are pressganged into working in the kitchen is: work hard at or pretend to be as bad a cook as can be and you'll never have to go near the kitchen again.

Jon Bannen
Actor

DON'T

My advice to cooks or anyone else is to get other people to do it for you.

The Duchess of Devonshire

CONSIDERATIONS

Botticelli isn't a wine, you Juggins! It's a cheese.

PUNCH

ORGANIZATION

Mise en place – literally, put in place – doing everything possible in advance – is the organizational dictum of the professional kitchen, and the single most important concept the private cook can take on board. Embrace it and your horizons will broaden, there will be more hours in the kitchen day and your execution will improve.

Richard Whittington
Writer and cook

PERFECTIONIST

Good cooking is the accumulation of small details, done to perfection.

Michel Bourdin
Chef de Cuisine, The Connaught Hotel, London

ONLY FOR LOVE

Never cook for people you don't like. Cooking is an art and every dish should be an offering, a labour of love. So if your husband wants to entertain his business people, or you feel you have to return hospitality to boring acquaintances, take them to a restaurant or get someone in to slave over the hot stove for you.

A. A. Gill
Food writer and journalist

BACK TO BASICS

Do not let us ever decry truly British traditional recipes – these are part of our national heritage. If the finest ingredients are used, and cooked simply and not over-ambitiously, you cannot fail to produce a worthwhile meal.

Francis Coulson
Chef and Proprietor, Sharrow Bay Hotel, Ullswater

BEFOREHAND

They say that time spent on reconnaissance is never wasted. When cooking, the time spent on choosing raw materials and in the preparation is never wasted.

Charles Campbell
Restaurateur

KEEP IT SIMPLE

Follow Escoffier's philosophy and 'make it simple'. Just concentrate on one good dish at a time – the perfect soup, the marvellous casserole, the most perfect pudding. Supplement with well-chosen bread, good cheese, salad, cream or whatever is needed. Even the greatest cooks find it difficult to produce a whole meal full of sparklers.

Mary Norwak
Food writer

HAPPY COOK

The secret of good and enjoyable cooking is not to be sparing with the wine – applied internally of course: before, during and after cooking. The result will invariably be satisfying to, at any rate, oneself: the opinions of others are, of course, of secondary importance.

Lord Aberconway

LOVING

Always keep your kitchen a homely, happy place to be. A loving kitchen produces wonderful food – always.

Germain Schwab
Patron, Winteringham Fields, South Humberside

GET YOUR MAN

Try to get a man to cook. Apart from professional chefs, cooking men seem to be regarded rather in the same light as walking dogs. It's not that they do it well but that they do it at all (apologies to Dr Johnson). A really average spaghetti bolognese, often involving a lot of tins, when concocted by a male, is frequently received by the assembled guests as one of the really great taste sensations of the twentieth century.

Nick Mason
Pink Floyd drummer and food enthusiast

ONLY THE BEST

Never pour into food what you can't pour down your throat.

Mary Ann Gilchrist
Head Chef, Carlton House, Llanwrtyd Wells

CHILDREN'S HOUR

Involve your children, especially in the preparation and cooking of vegetables. This will encourage them not only to eat more greens but also to understand the basics of cookery. Preparing a vegetable stew, you can do the peeling and scraping while they can wash and pop the various shapes and sizes into the pan, learning their names and, one hopes, getting to like them. It may take longer but is very worthwhile.

Denise Clarke

OUT OF BOUNDS

There are three rules in my kitchen, so that cooking is a relaxing experience for me.

1 No men allowed. Half the dinner will disappear before it is cooked, let alone served.
2 No children allowed. They will inevitably want something other than what you are cooking for dinner.
3 No 'helpful' mothers or mothers-in-law allowed. You will be told you are doing everything wrong.

Julie Anne Rhodes
Actress

COMFY

I have a sofa in my kitchen – it means that people

can talk to me as I cook, and I don't feel isolated.

The Hon. Mrs William Waldegrave

CONFIDENCE

Cooking, I find, is all about confidence. Two things help. First a really professional-looking apron, a touch grubby for extra effect. Second, a very large, stiff drink before you get started.

Rachel Cooke
Food writer, The Sunday Times

WHAT'S IN A NAME?

If a dish doesn't turn out right, change the name and don't bat an eyelid. A fallen soufflé is only a risen omelette. It depends on the self-confidence with which you present it.

Rabbi Lionel Blue

NOTHING VENTURED

Never be afraid of trying new recipes because you might fail. Often truly original ideas stem from failures.

Mike Womersley
Head Chef, Luckham Park, Colerne

LOOK BEFORE YOU COOK

Before you start cooking from a recipe it is worth spending a couple of minutes checking that you have all the ingredients. I know this sounds obvious but many are the times I have found that the butter I 'knew' I had has mysteriously disappeared. If you do get stuck half-way through the recipe and the crucial ingredient is missing, my advice is to experiment. Improvisation is wonderful – it's how cookery moves forward.

Nigel Slater
Food Editor, The Observer

179

COPYRIGHTS

If a friend is kind enough to give you the recipe for her favourite and unusual dish, try not to serve it back to her when she comes to dine with you. She won't be pleased. Similarly, keep it to yourself. She really will be sour if she dines with a mutual friend to find her precious 'Pork in port and pimento sauce' or whatever served up as 'just a little something I thought up myself'.

The Lady Wardington

THE SHORT VIEW

Advice to a young woman in low spirits from the Reverend Sydney Smith: take a short view of life – no further than dinner or tea.

Elisabeth Luard
Cookery columnist, The Scotsman

THE END

The French say that you never grow old at the table. This is salutary, profound and comforting, and as worthy of consideration each day as the thought that each day could be our last.

Richard Whittington
Writer and cook

INDEX OF HINTS

INDEX OF
CONTRIBUTORS